The Manhattan Diaries Series

Skyline Secrets
How Manhattan's Elite Tame Their Tresses

Manhattan Allure
Just Like That

The Manhattan Diaries Series

Manhattan Allure ~ Just Like That

Manhattan Vitality ~ Just Like That

Manhattan Lifestyle ~ Just Like That

Manhattan Ambition ~ Just Like That

The Manhattan Diaries Series

Skyline Secrets
How Manhattan's Elite Tame Their Tresses

Manhattan Allure
Just Like That

JESSICA BROOKS

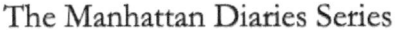

Urban Chronicles Publishing House
an imprint of The Ridge Publishing Group
Coeur d'Alene, Idaho, U.S.A.

DISCLAIMER: The ideas, concepts, and opinions expressed in The Manhattan Diaries Series (hereinafter referred to as "Series") are intended to help readers make thoughtful and informed decisions about their lifestyle. This Series is sold with the understanding that author and publisher are not rendering medical advice of any kind, nor is this Series intended to replace the medical advice, nor to diagnose, prescribe, or treat any disease, condition, illness, or injury. It should not be used as a substitute for treatment by or the advice of a professional healthcare provider. It is recommended that before beginning any diet or exercise program, including any aspect of the Series, you receive full medical clearance from a licensed healthcare provider. Although the author and publisher have endeavored to ensure that the information provided in the Series is complete and accurate, the author and publisher claim no responsibility to any person or entity for any liability, loss, or damage caused or alleged to be caused directly or indirectly as a result of the use, application, or interpretation of the material in this Series, or any errors or omissions in the Series.

CREDIT: This book was written with limited assistance of ChatGPT, an AI language model developed by OpenAI. The collaboration provided unique insights and support in crafting content. The book cover was created using Midjourney tools and Adobe Photoshop, ensuring a visually captivating design.

Library of Congress Control Number: 2024917644

Skyline Secrets: How Manhattan's Elite Tame Their Tresses by Jessica Brooks

ISBN: 978-1-956905-16-8 (e-book)
ISBN: 978-1-956905-15-1 (Softcover)

1. Health & Fitness / Beauty & Grooming. 2. Self-Help / Personal Growth / Success. 3. Self-Help / Motivational & Spiritual. 4. Lifestyle & Personal Style Guides. 5. Travel / United States / New York. I. Title. II. Series.

First Edition: September 2024

Contents

The Manhattan Diaries Series

DARE TO REIMAGINE YOURSELF . . .

21 Steps to Reinvent and Discover a Side of You Manhattan's Never Seen

The Manhattan Diaries Series presents:

Manhattan Allure—Just Like That mini-series (books 1–5)

Manhattan Vitality—Just Like That mini-series (books 6–10)

Manhattan Lifestyle—Just Like That mini-series (books 11–16)

Manhattan Ambition—Just Like That mini-series (books 17–21)

Meet the Author
https://www.LAMoeszinger.com

Meet the Publisher, Urban Chronicles Publishing House
https://www.NewYouniversityChronicles.com

Step into the whirlwind world of New York's glitzy underbelly, where the scintillating secrets and laugh-out-loud confessions of a metropolitan woman are laid bare by someone truly in the know. Through essays pulled from her chic "Manhattanite's Survival Guide—Success in the City," L invites us on an unforgettable strut from her glamorous youth, through her middle-aged mazes, and into her fabulous sixties.

For the juiciest tidbits about L's life, her "Manhattan Chronicles" blog is the place to be. This blog is an unfiltered dive into L's world, from her spiritual musings to her meticulous weigh-ins to her New Youniversity Chronicles—The Manhattan Diaries series—personal tales. Dive into her cosmos at her blog site: https://www.ManhattanChronicles.com.

The Manhattan Diaries Series

Skyline Secrets
How Manhattan's Elite Tame Their Tresses

Manhattan Allure
Just Like That

Introduction: Manhattan's Hair Affair – The Enchanting Elixir of Youth and Glamour!

Well, hello there, city connoisseurs! As you step out into the electrifying whirlwind of Manhattan, have you ever wondered how the elite of this metropolis keep their tresses effortlessly tamed amidst the chaos? Do you strut through the streets with the poise of a true New Yorker, or are you still decoding the mysteries of Manhattan's hair game? Well, dear reader, let me tell you, there's a world of secrets hidden behind those sleek, chic hairstyles, and I'm about to unveil them all in "Skyline Secrets: How Manhattan's Elite Tame Their Tresses."

In this captivating journey, I'm taking you on a behind-the-scenes tour of Manhattan's hair aristocracy. Success in New York City isn't just about wit or navigating the concrete canyons—it's about making a statement with your hair, a statement that turns heads at every fashionable event, from uptown soirees to downtown gatherings. I've mingled with the high society, attended the most exclusive galas, and discovered the hair secrets that keep Manhattan's finest looking their best. But remember, true confidence starts from within.

Consider this your golden ticket to a limited-edition of The Manhattan Diaries series, experience. Whether you devour this treasure trove over lazy days, savor it week by week, or read it while enjoying cocktails on Manhattan rooftops, the pace is entirely yours. Picture yourself diving into a chapter with your morning latte or immersing yourself in the entire book during a weekend getaway. Within these pages, you'll unlock the keys to becoming the master of your hair destiny, and the allure that follows will leave you spellbound.

As we embark on this journey together, I'll be your confidante, revealing how effortlessly you can conquer the realm of Manhattan's hair. This guide isn't just about hair tips; it's a rejuvenation of your spirit, your relationships, and your aspirations in the city. Join me in uncovering the secrets that will make your hair shine as brilliantly as the city skyline. I'm not just dedicated to helping you master the art of Manhattan hair; I'm here to ignite the confidence in your heart that propels you to your most captivating self. Embrace it, and the energy of New York will be yours to command!

My passion for this city-centric guide is born from my own personal journey, filled with highs and lows, passion and heartbreaks. Like many city dwellers, I had to blaze my own trail, sometimes veering off the well-trodden path. But today, I stand before you, ready to inspire you to conquer your city with your hair as your crown, cocktail in hand.

As time sails on the Hudson River, our life paths inevitably intersect. For me, the whirlwind of career pursuits, downtown extravaganzas, and self-discovery converged with my love for the city, leading me to work with the Urban Chronicles Publishing House.

New York City's allure isn't limited to celebrities or trust fund beneficiaries; it's accessible to everyone, whether you're a trendy twenty-something or a sophisticated sixty-something. Embrace this journey with me as we embark on a path to city stardom in this third step—The Manhattan Diaries series is a twenty-one step journey; twenty-one books to reinvent and discover a side of you Manhattan's never met.

"Skyline Secrets" equips you with the tools to not only dream big but to seize those dreams. I'm here as your city guardian, ensuring you realize that everything you crave starts within. With this guide, pamper your hair with Manhattan's finest secrets, and watch as your dream job, penthouse, or perfect partner follows suit. If you've got city-sized hair dreams, this series is your key to unlocking them! I've witnessed friends rise to hair stardom time and time again, proving that as you align within, the city will reflect it back in glitz and glamour. That's a promise straight from the heart of New York.

Relying on The Manhattan Diaries series has always been my lifeline. Whenever the city threw a curveball my way, this series steered me right back to my radiant path. The allure of always being on top keeps me coming back to these pages, and trust me, it's far more exhilarating than settling for mediocrity.

With every page you turn, you'll discover the blueprint, insider secrets, and the support you need to make your hair journey an exhilarating adventure. This series is tailored for everyone, from those seeking a fabulous career to social butterflies and empire builders.

There are countless ways to rise in the Big Apple, but if you're looking for the chicest route, it's right here in The Manhattan Diaries. Immerse yourself in its treasures while reciting positive mantras, and let the city's vibrancy chase away any doubts; and, in this case, allow your hair to become your ultimate statement piece. To truly reign, sometimes we need to shed our old hairstyles and embrace our most radiant selves.

Navigating the City with The Manhattan Diaries

Welcome to "Skyline Secrets: How Manhattan's Elite Tame Their Tresses." Think of this edition of The Manhattan Diaries as your personal cosmopolitan diary, as interactive as an invitation to Manhattan's most exclusive soirees. Each chapter is enriched with journal pages, waiting for your Manhattan musings and anecdotes. Whether you want to record the day's chic highlights in your "Hair Chronicles" or dive into deep reflections in your "Hair Confessions," these pages are yours to fill—see Cocktails and Chronicles: "Journal Pages: Pen Your Tales."

But . . .

✓ Before you start penning your thoughts, take a moment to breathe. Close your eyes, and in that quiet moment, express a heartfelt "thank you" to the city that never sleeps. Feel that rush of gratitude, as if you've just been given a front-row seat to New York Fashion Week. Let that "thank you" resonate deep within your heart—because that, my dear readers, is the magic of Manhattan.

2 Begin by detailing the fabulous strides you've made since delving into the last glamorous advice you've received. Write them down under "Your Triumphs," and relish in the feeling of owning every room you walk into with your stunning hair.

3 Once you've celebrated your hair triumphs, turn the page to "Your Goals" and outline your aspirations. Reflect on what's left to conquer in your hair journey, capturing your next steps in this transformational saga.

Throughout The Manhattan Diaries series, you'll encounter timeless "inspirational quotes" that are as iconic as Manhattan's skyline. These pearls of wisdom are your city mantras. Savor them, recite each word as if you're toasting at an Upper East Side salon, and let them resonate deep within your urban hair soul.

As you approach the end of each guide, you'll discover a "City Roundup." Here, you'll find a chic recap summarizing all the insider tips from your city escapade, ensuring you never miss a New York beauty minute.

So, prepare to unlock the secrets of Manhattan's hair elite in this edition of The Manhattan Diaries, darlings. Behind the skyline lies a world of glamour, style, and endless possibilities for your hair. It's time to let your hair shine as brightly as the city lights.

Skyline Secrets: How Manhattan's Elite Tame Their Tresses

Step into the enchanting world of Manhattan's elite once more with "Skyline Secrets: How Manhattan's Elite Tame Their Tresses," the third gem in The Manhattan Diaries series. Are you ready for the next step in achieving a truly extraordinary life? Well, darlings, it begins right here.

In "Skyline Secrets," you'll dive deep into the art of eternal youth—follicularly speaking, of course. Is your hair betraying your age? Fear not, for within these pages, you'll discover the secrets to defy time and keep your mane forever young.

Picture it: a radiant, lustrous mane that not only makes you look instantly healthy but also irresistibly attractive. Your hair can be your ultimate asset, and with the wisdom contained in this book, you'll unlock the key to a refined, ageless look that will turn heads on every bustling Manhattan street.

So, dear readers, get ready to embark on the next phase of your extraordinary life journey. Let "Skyline Secrets: How Manhattan's Elite Tame Their Tresses" be your guide to a timeless, youthful allure that will leave you feeling confident and unstoppable in the city that never sleeps.

Meet the Maestros Behind the Curtain

Welcome to the glittering realm of The Manhattan Diaries series, penned by an eclectic group of scribes who know how to make words shimmer just like that Midtown skyline. Each of these writers possesses the kind of Manhattan moxie that's as electrifying as a Saturday night at Studio 54. Picture the literary equivalent of the fabulous foursome from "Sex and the City," but with a little extra Manhattan mascara.

Our authors, darlings, aren't just writers; they're connoisseurs of all things NYC, dishing out stories with the precision of a Fifth Avenue stylist crafting the perfect blowout. Their tales are imbued with the kind of insider knowledge only those who've sipped martinis at the city's most secretive spots can truly understand.

So, as you delve into the pages of The Manhattan Diaries know that you're not just reading words, you're sipping on the prose of New York's finest literary mixologists. Here's to a journey as sparkling and unforgettable as a New York night out. Cheers, darling!

Behind the Scenes with the Urban Chronicles Publishing House

In the whirlwind of New York's high society, the Urban Chronicles Publishing House has emerged as the ultimate style sage for modern-day self-help. Over a cosmopolitan-fueled decade, they've become the city's go-to curators for crafting that sought-after, enviable life. The Manhattan Diaries? Envision it as your exclusive, VIP backstage pass, dripping with Upper East Side allure.

If you've ever pictured yourself sashaying through Manhattan with poise, if you've craved that skyline backdrop to your impeccable life, or if you simply seek the secrets whispered in the plush corners of the city's most exclusive clubs—The Manhattan Diaries is your ticket. Crafted under the elite banner, Urban Chronicles Publishing House, this imprint doesn't just offer you insights; it's your personal invite to the city's most glamorous circles.

- ➤ **Forever en Vogue.** Everyone, from the Wall Street moguls to the aspiring Broadway stars, dreams of basking in New York's radiant glow, of living a life drenched in style and substance. The wisdom in The Manhattan Diaries is as timeless as a Fifth Avenue romance, ensuring you're always en vogue.

- ➤ **A Blueprint for the Elite**. Nestled within these pages are the golden rules of city living, from mastering the cocktail chatter to undergoing a dazzling reinvention. Whether you're a seasoned socialite, an ambitious parent, or a fresh-eyed dreamer, these guides have something to make your heart race a little faster.

- ➤ **The Perfect Accessory**. Their petite stature makes these guides a seamless fit for your Prada clutch or your gym tote. Think of them as your urban survival kit—a blend of wisdom and wit that's as crucial as your red lipstick for those Manhattan nights.

Take a sip of this rich concoction, and let the Urban Chronicles Publishing House unlock Manhattan, unveiling a New York you only dreamed of. Welcome to the allure of the elite, darling.

Unveiling The Ridge Publishing Group

Picture The Ridge Publishing Group as the rising star on New York's literary and entertainment horizon. Envision an eclectic empire—books, cinema, and board games—setting the stage to become the world's haute couture of theological discourse. Think Fifth Avenue for theological resources: luxurious, elite, and unparalleled.

Dive into their esteemed collections. They hold the keys to the illustrious Guardians of Biblical Truth Publishing Group and the evocative New Narrated Study Bible (NNSB) series. Delve deeper and find the Hoyle Theology Publishing Group and its opulent Hoyle Theology Encyclopedia—a treasure trove for the cerebral sophisticate. And for those who like their theology paired with a cinematic flair, there's the Documentaries in Print Publishing Group with its tantalizing series like Defending the Faith. And, of course, for those cocktail nights with a side of divine strategy, the Heaven's Seminary board games and card decks offer a chic twist.

But that's not all. The Ridge Publishing Group is more than a theological publishing powerhouse; it's a brand. Alongside its flagship, it flaunts trendy imprints: AuthorsDoor Group and AuthorsDoor Leadership (check them out at the glamorous digital boulevard of https://www.AuthorsDoor.com), the ritzy Urban Chronicles Publishing House and New Youniversity (make your reservation at https://www.LAMoeszinger.com), and the novel delights of Ethan Fox Books (sip your martini and browse https://www.EthanFox Books.com).

For a sneak peek into the world where theology meets Manhattan glamour, rendezvous at their digital penthouse: https://www.Ridge PublishingGroup.com. It's theology made chic.

A NOTE TO THE READER

Typos in this book? Errors (and inconsistencies) can get through proofreaders, so if you do find any typos or grammatical errors in this book, I'd be very grateful if you could let me know using this email address typos@LAMoeszinger.com. Thank you ☺

High-Rise Hairdos: Secrets from Penthouse Salons

Manhattan, a city that doesn't merely witness trends—it births them, as each shimmering silhouette against the skyline tells tales of audacity, creativity, and the undeniable chase for perfection. In this city of sky-touching dreams, it's not just about who you are, but how you frame yourself—with elegance, flair, and the inevitable high-rise twist.

Now imagine: Your sweeping through Central Park West, and while the whispers marvel at your chic ensemble, it's the gravity-defying grace of your hair that commands the room. That, darling, is the Manhattan Crown of Glory, a statement that doesn't just rest atop your head, but one that encapsulates the city's aspirational spirit.

In this tantalizing chapter of The Manhattan Diaries, we elevate ourselves to the pinnacle of beauty—the illustrious penthouse salons, where the city's mavens get their manes tamed and teased. From the wind-swept, balcony-breeze waves to the sleek uptown bun, you'll unlock the secrets to hair that not only touches the sky but seems birthed from it.

But this isn't merely about strands and styles. It's about understanding the architectural wonder that is Manhattan, crafting tresses that tell a story, that encapsulate an ambition, an identity, a legacy. It's about drawing inspiration from the skyscraper's majestic rise and the horizons they dare to challenge.

Join me, as we ascend to the top floors of beauty, imbibing in the expertise of stylist who don't just see hair, but see art, potential, and skyline. Because, precious, in Manhattan, every hairdo is a personal blueprint of dreams. Style your tresses, for the city beckons with a challenge. Welcome to The Manhattan Diaries—where your hair mirrors the city's upward ambition.

The Penthouse Salon Experience

Darlings, get ready to step into a world where glamour knows no bounds—the unparalleled Penthouse Salon Experience. Imagine yourself whisked away to a luxurious oasis high above the bustling streets of Manhattan, where opulence and beauty converge to transform you into the epitome of urban chic. With its panoramic views of the city, personalized pampering, and a team of top-tier stylists at your disposal, this is the ultimate indulgence for those who demand nothing but the best. So, slip into your designer ensemble, and let's take a ride to the penthouse of perfection.

> ➤ **Elevator to Elegance**. Begin your journey with a private elevator ride that whisks you straight to The Penthouse Salon's grand entrance, ensuring your arrival is as elevated as your aspirations.

> ➤ **Meet the Maestro**. Monsieur Fabien, the salon's artistic director, welcomes you with a glass of vintage champagne. His discerning eye and French savoir-faire make him the mastermind behind your transformation. Fabien will consult with you to craft a bespoke beauty plan, ensuring your look is uniquely tailored to your style and personality.

> ➤ **Artistry Unleashed**. The salon's team of skilled stylists, colorists, and makeup artists work in perfect harmony to execute Fabien's vision. While your hair is artfully sculpted, indulge in a heavenly massage that rivals the finest spas, leaving you feeling relaxed and rejuvenated.

> ➤ **Beyond Hair**. The Penthouse Salon isn't merely a hair haven; it's an oasis of overall beauty. Expert estheticians pamper you with luxurious facials and rejuvenating treatments, followed by flawless makeup application. You'll leave exuding the radiance and confidence of a true Manhattan icon.

➢ **Terrace of Tranquility**. Enjoy exclusive access to the salon's private terrace, where you can luxuriate in the sun with breathtaking skyline views while your hair dries naturally. Sip on a mimosa and relish in the gentle breeze for the ultimate relaxation.

➢ **Concierge Elegance**. The salon's personalized concierge service leaves no detail unattended. From arranging chauffeured luxury transportation to fulfilling your every desire, whether it's a gourmet lunch or a rare vintage wine, you'll be treated like royalty.

➢ **Guardians of Privacy**. Discretion is paramount at The Penthouse Salon, with walls adorned by framed photos of celebrity clientele who value their privacy as much as their impeccable appearances. Rest assured that your secrets are held in the strictest confidence.

➢ **Gift of Glamour**. Before your departure, receive a custom-designed gift bag filled with the salon's signature haircare products and beauty essentials. This ensures that your fabulous look is effortlessly maintained, allowing you to carry a piece of Manhattan's elite beauty culture with you.

➢ **Signature Scents and Sounds**. As you step into the salon, be enveloped by the salon's signature scent, a custom blend of aromas designed to uplift and inspire. Meanwhile, a curated playlist of soothing and stylish music complements the luxurious atmosphere, setting the perfect tone for a day of unparalleled pampering.

As your Penthouse Salon Experience draws to a close, you'll emerge from this sanctuary feeling like the star of your own Manhattan story. Your hair, your makeup, your aura—everything about you will reflect the essence of the city that never sleeps. So, my darlings, if you crave the epitome of pampering and glamour, make your reservation at The Penthouse Salon and embark on a journey that will leave you transformed and ready to conquer the world. After all, every day is a red-carpet moment waiting to happen.

Completed Tasks: Salon Experience Activities

_____
_____
_____
_____
_____
_____
_____
_____
_____
_____
_____
_____
_____
_____
_____
_____
_____
_____
_____
_____
_____
_____
_____
_____
_____
_____
_____
_____

WE RELISH NEWS OF OUR HEROES, FORGETTING THAT WE ARE EXTRAORDINARY TO SOMEBODY TOO. — Helen Hayes

Action Items: Intentions and Thoughts

Architectural Inspiration in Hairstyling

Darlings, today we're delving into a realm where artistry meets architecture, where hairstyling becomes an exquisite form of self-expression inspired by the grandeur of our city's iconic structures. Yes, I'm talking about the enchanting world of Architectural Inspiration in Hairstyling. Just like the skyscrapers that pierce the New York skyline, these visionary stylists use their scissors and brushes to create hair masterpieces that are nothing short of architectural marvels. So, fasten your seatbelts, my darlings, as we embark on a tour of hairdos that would make the Guggenheim proud and hairstyles that reach new heights of sophistication.

- ➢ **Empire Elegance**. Behold the Empire State Building's grace and grandeur translated into a hairstyle. With its sleek lines and Art Deco charm, this look exudes timeless elegance, perfect for red carpet events and gala soirees.

- ➢ **Gothic Glamour**. Picture the intricate details of a gothic cathedral reimagined in hair. This style combines elaborate braids and twists, reminiscent of the cathedral's spires and arches, creating a look that's equal parts mystical and majestic.

- ➢ **Modernist Minimalism**. Inspired by the minimalist aesthetic of contemporary architecture, this hairstyle features clean lines and a sleek, polished finish. It's the epitome of chic simplicity, ideal for the modern woman on the move.

- ➢ **Suspension Bridge Strands**. Channeling the strength and structure of our city's suspension bridges, this hairstyle features bold, angular layers that defy gravity. It's a striking look that's bound to turn heads on any occasion.

- ➢ **Art Deco Revival**. Transport yourself to the roaring '20s with a hairstyle inspired by the opulent Art Deco era. Think sleek waves, finger curls, and glitzy accessories that capture the spirit of the Chrysler Building's gleaming spire.

➢ **Brownstone Elegance**. Channel the timeless charm of New York's brownstone architecture with a hairstyle that's as classic as it is chic. Soft, cascading curls and a polished updo pay homage to the brownstone stoops that line our city's streets.

➢ **Skyline Silhouette**. Imagine the Manhattan skyline at dusk—now envision it in your hair. This avant-garde style uses precise cutting techniques to recreate the city's iconic skyscrapers, resulting in a look that's both bold and breathtaking.

➢ **Lofty Loft Vibes**. Capture the essence of loft living with a hairstyle that's effortlessly cool and edgy. Layers and texture mimic the exposed brick and beams found in SoHo's iconic lofts, giving you a style that's as dynamic as the city itself.

➢ **Bridge to Brilliance**. Pay homage to our city's bridges with a hairstyle that blends strength and elegance. This look combines structured braids with flowing waves, echoing the graceful arches and sturdy cables of our iconic bridges.

As our tour through the world of Architectural Inspiration in Hairstyling comes to a close, remember that just as architects shape the skyline, hairstylists sculpt and define our personal style. These visionary artisans take their inspiration from the very heart of our city, infusing it into every strand of hair. So, my darlings, when you're ready to make a statement and turn heads with a hairstyle that's a work of art, seek out these architectural hair maestros. In the world of The Manhattan Diaries, your hair isn't just a canvas; it's a masterpiece waiting to be unveiled.

Completed Tasks: Architectural Inspiration Activities

_____
_____
_____
_____
_____
_____

HAPPINESS IS A BUTTERFLY, WHICH WHEN PURSUED IS ALWAYS JUST BEYOND YOUR GRASP, BUT WHICH IF YOU WILL SIT DOWN QUIETLY, MAY ALIGHT UPON YOU. — Nathaniel Hawthorne

Action Items: Intentions and Thoughts

Trends Set High Above the Street

Darlings, have you ever wondered how the streets of Manhattan come to life with the latest fashion trends? Well, let me take you high above those bustling streets to where the magic begins—the world of Trends Set High Above the Street. From penthouse soirees to rooftop runways, this is where fashion visionaries and style influencers gather to shape the very essence of New York's sartorial landscape. So, put on your most glamorous outfit, grab your oversized shades, and join me on a journey into the chicest, most elevated fashion scene in the city.

> ➢ **Penthouse Pioneers.** Meet the designers who host exclusive fashion previews and trunk shows in their penthouses, offering an intimate look at their latest collections against a backdrop of panoramic skyline views.

> ➢ **Rooftop Runways.** Picture fashion shows high above the city streets, where models strut their stuff on helipads and terraces, showcasing avant-garde designs that challenge the status quo and redefine the fashion landscape.

> ➢ **Skyline Soirees.** Imagine attending exclusive rooftop soirees, where the city's trendsetters gather to discuss the latest fashion obsessions. These gatherings offer a sneak peek into the hottest styles and are the perfect backdrop for networking with style mavens.

> ➢ **Rooftop Retail Therapy.** Some of the city's most exclusive boutiques set up pop-up shops on rooftop terraces, allowing fashion enthusiasts to shop for limited-edition pieces while taking in breathtaking views.

> ➢ **High-Flying Influencers.** Influencers and fashion bloggers ascend to the skies for photo shoots against the cityscape, setting the stage for the next viral trend that will flood your social media feeds.

➢ **Fashion-Fueled Helicopter Tours**. Picture helicopter tours that highlight the city's architectural beauty and fashion landmarks, giving you a bird's-eye view of the most stylish corners of Manhattan.

➢ **Culinary Couture**. Rooftop restaurants are not just about the cuisine; they're also showcases for fashion-forward dining experiences. Imagine dining while models strut in the latest designer attire, merging the worlds of gastronomy and style.

➢ **Sky-High Launch Parties**. Step into exclusive launch parties held in sky-high venues, where new fashion lines are unveiled amid the glittering lights of the city. These events are a mix of glamour, innovation, and celebration, attended by fashion elites and celebrities.

➢ **Designer Workshops in the Clouds**. Participate in unique, hands-on workshops led by renowned designers on scenic rooftops. These sessions offer insights into the creative process and the art of fashion design, providing a rare opportunity to learn from the best while surrounded by the city's inspiring vistas.

➢ **Starlit Style Debates**. Engage in spirited discussions and debates about fashion's hottest topics under the stars. Hosted by industry experts, these debates cover everything from sustainability in fashion to the impact of technology on design, providing food for thought is a truly inspiring setting.

As our journey through the world of Trends Set High Above the Street comes to an end, remember that fashion in New York is more than just clothing; it's a lifestyle, an attitude, and a constant evolution. It's about capturing the essence of the city and making a statement that's as bold as the skyline itself. So, my darlings, embrace the fashion highlife, and let the streets of Manhattan become your personal runway. In the word of The Manhattan Diaries, style is not just a trend; it's an art form, and the city is your muse.

Completed Tasks: Hair Topic and Trend Activities

Inspirational Quote

NOBLE DEEDS THAT ARE CONCEALED ARE MOST ESTEEMED. — Blaise Pascal

Action Items: Intentions and Thoughts

The Masters Behind the Manes

Darlings, gather 'round, because I've got a juicy tale to tell you about the masters behind the manes, those unsung heroes who sculpt and style the luscious locks of the city's most glamorous residents. Just like a well-crafted cocktail, the secrets to these mane magicians' success are mixed with a dash of mystery, a splash of talent, and a whole lot of attitude. So, slip into your favorite pair of stilettos, darlings, and let's dive into the world of the hair whisperers who make Manhattan's elite look like they've stepped straight out of a Vogue editorial.

➢ **Dante Santangelo: The Uptown Elegance Maestro**. Picture a tall, dark, and brooding Italian with a pair of scissors in one hand and a glass of champagne in the other. Dante is the mastermind behind the manes of the Upper East Side's socialites. He's the go-to guy for perfectly tousled beach waves that scream "I woke up like this." His salon is a haven of luxury, where you can sip on cappuccinos and gossip about last night's soiree while he works his magic.

➢ **Ruby Sparks: The Downtown Daredevil Stylist**. Next up is the irreverent Ruby Sparks. She's not your typical hairstylist. With her candy-colored hair and an affinity for leopard print, Ruby is the queen of the downtown scene. Her clients include rockstars, artists, and the edgiest of the fashion elite. She's known for her avant-garde creations, from neon buzz cuts to asymmetrical, punk-inspired styles that are as daring as they are fabulous.

➢ **Fae Summers: The Enigmatic Extension Enchanter**. And let's not forget the enigmatic Fae Summers. She's the mysterious sorceress of hair extensions, making locks reach lengths that defy logic and gravity. Fae's salon, tucked away in a discreet corner of the city, is frequented by A-list celebrities who trust her to keep their hair looking flawless. Rumor has it she's got a secret formula for extensions that can withstand even the wildest parties.

➢ **Xavier Beaumont: The Wall Street Mane Maestro**. In the glittering metropolis of Manhattan, Xavier Beaumont is the charismatic coiffure conductor of Wall Street's elite. With a clientele that includes hedge fund moguls and CEOs, Xavier is the man to see for impeccable power cuts that exude confidence and authority. His salon is a hushed oasis in the financial district, where deals are made and secrets are kept.

➢ **Celeste Sterling: The Upper West Side Color Virtuoso**. Don't forget about the color genius of the Upper West Side, Celeste Sterling. Her Midas touch with hair dyes and highlights has earned her a reputation as the go-to guru for natural-looking transformations. Celeste's salon is a tranquil escape from the chaos of city life, where clients leave with hair that glistens like the sun setting over Central Park.

➢ **Rex Vidal: The Celebrity Stylist to the Stars**. Rex Vidal is the go-to celebrity stylist for A-list names. As a result, Rex knows how to make every client feel like Hollywood royalty.

In the world of Manhattan, these hair artisans aren't just stylists; they're the gatekeepers of glamour, the custodians of confidence, and the whisperers of wishes. Their salons are sanctuaries where dreams are woven into hair, and every client leaves feeling like the star of their own show.

So there you have it, my darlings, the Masters Behind the Manes, the unsung heroes who turn ordinary tresses into extraordinary works of art. Whether you're uptown or downtown, their scissors, brushes, and magical potions are waiting to transform you into the epitome of Manhattan chic. Go forth and conquer the city with the fiercest, most fabulous hair, because in the world of The Manhattan Diaries, there's nothing a great hair day can't fix.

SKYLINE SECRETS

Completed Tasks: Hair Whisperers Activities

Inspirational Quote

IF A MAN DOES NOT KEEP PACE WITH HIS COMPANIONS PERHAPS IT IS BECAUSE HE HEARS A DIFFERENT DRUMMER. LET HIM STEP TO THE MUSIC WHICH HE HEARS, HOWEVER MEASURED OR FAR AWAY. — Henry David Thoreau

26

Action Items: Intentions and Thoughts

Hair as a Symbol of Personal Evolution

Darlings, let's dive deep into a world where hair isn't just strands of silk; it's a canvas of personal evolution. Yes, you heard me right—hair as a symbol of personal growth and transformation. Picture this: the way we style, cut, or color our hair can be a reflection of our inner journey, a manifestation of our desires and aspirations. So, slip into your most stylish attire and join me on a journey into the fascinating realm of Hair as a Symbol of Personal Evolution.

➢ **The Chop Heard Round the World: A Fresh Start**. Sometimes, a dramatic haircut can signify a fresh beginning. That bold pixie cut or edgy buzz says, "I'm shedding the old, embracing the new, and daring to be different."

➢ **Color Me Bold: Expressing Individuality**. Transforming your hair color can be an act of self-expression. Whether it's going platinum blonde, fiery red, or a mermaid-worthy shade of blue, it's about showcasing your uniqueness to the world.

➢ **From Long Locks to Short Sensation: Liberation and Reinvention**. Trading in long locks for a chic short style can symbolize liberation and reinvention. It's about letting go of the past and embracing a future filled with confidence and independence.

➢ **Embracing Gray and Grace: Authenticity and Wisdom**. For some, embracing natural gray hair is a symbol of authenticity and wisdom. It's a declaration that they've earned every silver strand, and they wear it with pride.

➢ **The Long and Short of It: Confidence and Empowerment**. Transitioning from short to long hair, or vice versa, can signify a journey of self-discovery and empowerment. It's about finding your unique style and owning it with confidence.

➢ **Au Naturel: Embracing Authenticity**. Opting for a natural, untouched look can symbolize a commitment to authenticity and self-acceptance. It's a statement that says, "I am beautiful just as I am."

➢ **Braids of Strength: Overcoming Challenges**. Intricate braids can be a symbol of strength and resilience. They tell a story of overcoming obstacles and weaving together the threads of one's life into a beautiful tapestry.

➢ **The Rebel Bob: Breaking Free**. Choosing a rebellious bob haircut can signify a break from convention and societal norms. It's about defying expectations and carving out your path on your terms.

➢ **The Playful Ponytail: Embracing Youthful Joy**. A bouncy, carefree ponytail can represent a return to youthful joy and spontaneity. It's a declaration that you're not taking life too seriously and savoring the moments of fun and playfulness.

➢ **Curls of Complexity: Embracing the Twists of Life**. Sporting natural curls or choosing to curl your straight hair can signify embracing the complexities and unpredictability of life. Each curl, unique in its form and bounce, represents the twists and turns of your journey, reminding you and the world that beauty often lies in not knowing what comes next but embracing it all the same.

As our journey through the world of Hair as a Symbol of Personal Evolution comes to a close, remember that the way you wear your hair can be a powerful statement of who you are and where you're headed. It's a manifestation of your journey, your experiences, and your aspirations. So, darlings, let your hair be the canvas upon which you paint your personal story, and wear it with the confidence and grace of a New Yorker on a mission to conquer the world. In the world of The Manhattan Diaries, every hairstyle is a chapter in the book of life, and each one is more intriguing than the last.

Completed Tasks: Hair Journey Activities

_____
_____
_____
_____
_____
_____
_____
_____
_____
_____
_____
_____
_____
_____
_____
_____
_____
_____
_____
_____
_____
_____
_____
_____
_____
_____
_____

Inspirational Quote

MY MISSION IN LIFE IS NOT MERELY TO SURVIVE, BUT TO THRIVE; AND TO DO SO WITH SOME PASSION, SOME COMPASSION, SOME HUMOR, AND SOME STYLE. — Maya Angelou

Action Items: Intentions and Thoughts

Action Items: Intentions and Thoughts

Fifth Avenue Follies:
The Truth About Those Lustrous Locks

Manhattan, a city that doesn't just see people—it gazes deep into their souls, deciphering the stories interwoven into every curl, twist, and tangle of hair. Here, in this sprawling urban landscape, it isn't just about walking the talk; it's about flaunting those locks—with elegance, sophistication, and a hint of Fifth Avenue mischief.

Now imagine: You're sashaying down Fifth Avenue, and while many are beguiled by the sway of your dress, it's the cascading sheen of your hair that leaves an indelible mark. That, my dear, is the Manhattan Hair Affair, an enigma that goes beyond the mere aesthetics, capturing hearts and turning heads.

In this enticing chapter of The Manhattan Diaries, we unfurl the tales behind those coveted Fifth Avenue tresses. From the late-night emergency trims in dimly lit penthouses to the champagne-infused deep conditioning rituals, you'll be privy to secrets that make those locks the crowning glory of Manhattan's elite.

Yet this is more than just about hair—it's a statement, a proclamation. It's about flowing with the rhythm of Fifth Avenue's bustling beat, each strand narrating tales of rendezvous, of dreams realized and aspirations yet to be achieved. It's about the juxtaposition of Manhattan's gloss and its gritty underbelly, manifesting in every hair flip and gentle tousle.

So come along, as we delve deep into the salons where magic is spun, one hair strand at a time. For in Manhattan, every hair tells a story, every curl holds a secret. Style them right, and the city might just share its hidden tales with you. Welcome to The Manhattan Diaries—where your hair's shimmer rivals the glint of the city lights.

Introduction to Manhattan's Hair Affair

Darlings, gather 'round, for today we embark on a journey into the heart of Manhattan's most enigmatic affair—the affair of hair. In this sprawling urban wonderland where glamour and ambition intertwine, where every street is a runway and every corner a scene, one thing is clear: hair is more than mere adornment. It's a statement, an expression, a canvas upon which the stories of this city's elite are woven. So, slip into your most dazzling ensemble, my darlings, and join me as we delve into the captivating world of Introduction to Manhattan's Hair Affair.

➢ **The Runway Called Streets**. Envision the grandeur of Manhattan's bustling avenues as more than mere thoroughfares. They are the runways where every resident becomes a fashion icon. With each step, the city is their audience, and their hair serves as the piece de resistance of their personal style. In this urban theater of style and elegance, every outing becomes a chance to flaunt their individuality and creativity, transforming sidewalks into glamorous catwalks.

➢ **The Art of Mane Manifesto**. In Manhattan, hairstyling transcends mere grooming—it becomes an art form and a manifesto of personal identity. Residents here embrace the opportunity to express their unique personalities through their hair, turning every strand into a masterpiece. The city's diversity fosters an environment where bold experimentation and avant-garde styles are not only accepted but celebrated. Hair becomes a powerful medium for conveying one's passions, beliefs, and innermost desires.

➢ **Hair Chronicles of a City**. In the city that never sleeps, every hair strand holds a story. These stories weave together to create a rich tapestry of life experiences, chronicling the journey of each resident. From dramatic makeovers to subtle transformations, hair captures moments of triumph, love, heartache, and personal growth. It becomes a silent witness to the vibrant tapestry of Manhattan's diverse and ever-evolving populace.

➢ **From Penthouses to Pavements**. The versatility of Manhattan's hairstyles is a testament to the city's multifaceted nature. On the upper floors of luxurious penthouses, elegance and sophistication reign supreme. Sleek updos and flawless waves grace the heads of the elite. Yet, as you descend to the vibrant streets, you encounter a charmingly disheveled elegance, where effortless bedhead looks and creative chaos rule the day. Manhattan's hair mirrors the contrasting worlds of high society and artistic Bohemia.

➢ **Hair, The Crown of Manhattan**. In this captivating city, hair isn't just an accessory; it's the crown that reigns over the grand narrative of life, love, and ambition. It's the embodiment of one's personal journey, an expression of their aspirations and dreams. Like a crown, it symbolizes authority, individuality, and the power to conquer the world's most iconic metropolis.

➢ **Gloss and Grit, in Every Strand**. And finally, let's uncover the spellbinding contrast that defines Manhattan—the glossy veneer of its exterior juxtaposed with the grit of its underbelly, with every hair flip, tousle, and subtle twist holding this captivating duality.

As we conclude our Introduction to Manhattan's Hair Affair, remember that in this city, your hair isn't just a canvas; it's a living narrative, an ode to your journey, your dreams, and your unique individuality. Embrace the allure of Manhattan's hair affair, where your locks don't just shine, they illuminate your path amid the city lights. In the world of The Manhattan Diaries, every strand has a story, and the city is the stage for your most captivating performance. So, darlings, let your hair be the embodiment of your tale, and let Manhattan be your ever-inspiring muse.

Completed Tasks: Hair Affair Activities

Inspirational Quote

WHEN YOU GET INTO A TIGHT PLACE AND EVERYTHING GOES AGAINST YOU, TILL IT SEEMS AS THOUGH YOU COULD NOT HANG ON A MINUTE LONGER, NEVER GIVE UP THEN, FOR THAT IS JUST THE PLACE AND TIME THAT THE TIDE WILL TURN. — Harriet Beecher Stowe

Action Items: Intentions and Thoughts

The Secrets of Manhattan's Elite Hair

Darlings, let us now venture deep into the inner sanctums of Manhattan's elite, where locks of hair are not just strands but secrets, where the pursuit of perfection is an art form, and where the maintenance of exquisite tresses is nothing short of a clandestine affair. Yes, my dear friends, welcome to The Secrets of Manhattan's Elite Hair, a realm where glamour knows no bounds, and the pursuit of the perfect coiffure is nothing short of an obsession.

- ➢ **The Penthouse Elegance**. Delve into the world of Manhattan's penthouses, where hair maintenance reaches new heights. The elite have their locks attended to in the privacy of luxurious penthouses, far from the prying eyes of the city below.

- ➢ **Champagne-Infused Rituals**. Explore the champagne-infused deep conditioning rituals that have become a hallmark of Manhattan's elite. These opulent treatments not only nourish the hair but also offer a lavish indulgence that is the envy of all.

- ➢ **The Midnight Trims**. Unveil the world of late-night emergency trims, where skilled stylists arrive at dimly lit penthouses, armed with shears and expertise, to ensure that not a strand is out of place, even in the wee hours.

- ➢ **Celebrity Whispers**. Peek behind the curtain to discover the hush-hush exchanges between Manhattan's elite and their celebrity stylists. These relationships are built on trust, discretion, and the promise of red carpet-worthy locks.

- ➢ **Hair as a Status Symbol**. In Manhattan, hair is not just an accessory; it's a status symbol. Explore how having impeccably styled locks is a declaration of one's position in the city's hierarchy, a silent statement that resonates through the concrete jungle.

➢ **The Stylist's Oath of Silence**. Explore the unspoken pact between Manhattan's elite and their stylists, where discretion in the ultimate currency. These trusted confidants guard not only the secrets of impeccable hair but also the intimate tales shared behind salon doors.

➢ **Hair-itage of Excellence**. Delve into the hair-itage of excellence in Manhattan's elite hair circles, where salons aren't merely places of grooming but historical institutions. Generations of families entrust their locks to these revered establishments, passing down the legacy of impeccable hair care.

➢ **The Intricate Dance of Extensions**. Unveil the fascinating world of hair extensions, where natural and artificial locks blend seamlessly to create voluminous, envy-inducing tresses. This artistry allows Manhattan's elite to switch effortlessly between styles with an air of effortless glamour.

➢ **The Power of a Signature Style**. Examine how Manhattan's elite often cultivate a signature hairstyle that becomes their unmistakable hallmark. These iconic looks are meticulously maintained, embodying the essence of personal brand and influence.

As we conclude our journey into The Secrets of Manhattan's Elite Hair, remember that in this world, every strand is a precious thread, every hair appointment a clandestine rendezvous, and every style a piece of art. The pursuit of perfection knows no bounds, and Manhattan's elite understand that maintaining flawless hair is not a choice but a way of life. In the world of The Manhattan Diaries, we've uncovered the mysteries and decadence that surround Manhattan's most coveted tresses. So, my darlings, let your hair be the embodiment of opulence, and let Manhattan be your playground as you embrace the secrets that lie within its elite hair circles.

Completed Tasks: Signature Hairstyle Activities

_____

_____

_____

_____

_____

_____

_____

_____

_____

_____

_____

_____

_____

_____

_____

_____

_____

_____

_____

_____

_____

_____

_____

_____

_____

_____

Inspirational Quote

I AM NOT AFRAID OF TOMORROW, FOR I HAVE SEEN YESTERDAY, AND I LOVE TODAY! — William Allen White

Action Items: Intentions and Thoughts

Hair as a Manhattan Proclamation

Darlings, in the enchanting labyrinth of Manhattan, hair isn't just an adornment; it's a proclamation. It's a statement of identity, an expression of personal growth, aspirations, and the exquisite journey of self-discovery. Today, we embark on a journey into the soul of the city as we explore Hair as a Manhattan Proclamation, where every strand becomes a narrative, and every hairstyle is a reflection of ambition and individuality.

➢ **The Tresses of Ambition**. Understand how, in the heart of Manhattan, hair isn't just an adornment; it's a proclamation. It's a proclamation to the world that you are here, you are determined, and you are ready to conquer the concrete jungle.

➢ **The Elegance of Aspiration**. Explore the notion that hair in Manhattan isn't just about looking good; it's about embodying the elegance of one's aspirations. It's a canvas on which dreams are painted, and every strand tells a story of what could be.

➢ **Hair, The Ever-Evolving Art**. Unveil the dynamic nature of hairstyles in Manhattan—a city where reinvention is a way of life. Hairstyles change with the seasons, just as dreams and ambitions evolve with time.

➢ **The Bond Between Hair and Personality**. Examine how Manhattan's residents forge a profound connection between their hair and their personalities. Each hairstyle is carefully curated to reflect an aspect of their multifaceted selves.

➢ **A City of Reinvention**. Highlight the essence of Manhattan as a city of reinvention, where residents are encouraged to express themselves through their ever-evolving hairstyles. It's a place where your hair doesn't just frame your face; it frames your journey.

➤ **Hair as a Cityscape**. Delve into the concept that in Manhattan, hair becomes a microcosm of the city itself. Just as the skyline evolves, so do hairstyles, reflecting the ever-changing nature of life in the city.

➤ **The Language of Locks**. Examine how, in Manhattan, hair becomes a language all its own—a silent communicator of confidence, ambition, and attitude. Each style carries a unique message to the world.

➤ **The Salon as a Sanctuary**. Unveil the role of salons as sanctuaries of self-expression in the city. These hallowed spaces are where Manhattanites come to transform not only their hair but also their sense of self.

➤ **Manhattan's Diverse Mane Manifestos**. Explore the diversity of hair expressions in Manhattan, where residents draw inspiration from a myriad of cultures and subcultures, resulting in a tapestry of styles that celebrate individuality.

➤ **Manhattan's Diverse Mane Manifestos**. Explore the diversity of hair expressions in Manhattan, where residents draw inspiration from a myriad of cultures and subcultures, resulting in a tapestry of styles that celebrate individuality.

As we conclude our exploration of Hair as a Manhattan Proclamation, remember that in this city, every strand is a proclamation of who you are and who you aspire to be. It's a testament to your ambition, resilience, and the ever-unfolding chapters of your life. In the world of The Manhattan Diaries, we've uncovered the narrative that exists within each hairstyle, the dreams that adorn every lock, and the spirit of reinvention that defines Manhattan. So, my darlings, let your hair be your proclamation, and let the city be your canvas as you boldly declare your presence in this remarkable metropolis.

Completed Tasks: Hair Proclamation Activities

_____

_____

_____

_____

_____

_____

_____

_____

_____

_____

_____

_____

_____

_____

_____

_____

_____

_____

_____

_____

_____

_____

_____

_____

_____

_____

_____

Inspirational Quote

I BELIEVE EVERY HUMAN HAS A FINITE NUMBER OF HEARTBEATS. I DON'T INTEND TO WASTE ANY OF MINE. — Neil Armstrong

Action Items: Intentions and Thoughts

The Salons of Manhattan's Magic

Darlings, in the shimmering heart of Manhattan, where dreams are woven into reality, there exists a sanctuary—a place where the alchemy of beauty and transformation unfolds. These are the salons of Manhattan's magic, where hair is not merely styled, but where stories are whispered, and personal metamorphosis occurs. Join me as we embark on a journey into The Salons of Manhattan's Magic, where each visit is a sojourn into the world of self-reinvention and elegance.

➤ **The Sanctuaries of Transformation**. Explore how Manhattan's salons are more than just places to get your done—they are sanctuaries of transformation. Within these hallowed halls, residents entrust skilled artisans with their locks and their aspirations.

➤ **The Artistry of the Chair**. Delve into the intimacy between client and stylist, as the salon chair becomes a throne of artistry. It's here that Manhattan's elite share their dreams, desires, and the vision of their next signature look.

➤ **Echoes of Elegance in Every Snip**. Discover the symphony of style where each snip at Manhattan's salons not only transform looks but also boosts confidence, making each visit a key step in personal reinvention

➤ **The Ritual of Self-Care**. Uncover the rituals of self-care that unfold within these salons. From soothing scalp massages to impeccable grooming, these rituals are a testament to the importance of pampering oneself in a city that never stops.

➤ **The City's Hidden Tales**. Highlight the notion that in these salons, the city's hidden tales are unveiled. It's where confidential exchanges take place, secrets are revealed, and where the dreams and aspirations of Manhattanites come to life, one strand at a time.

- ➢ **The Masterpieces of Manhattan**. Examine how Manhattan's salons are more than just places for hair—it's where masterpieces are created. Skilled stylists sculpt hair into works of art, crafting personalized styles that become the crowning glory of their clients.

- ➢ **Salon as a Social Hub**. Explore how Manhattan's salons aren't just places for hair; they are social hubs where friendships are forged, alliances are made, and where the city's elite come to see and be seen.

- ➢ **The Aura of Artistry**. Delve into the aura of artistry that envelopes these salons, where stylists aren't just professionals but true artists. They craft hairstyles that not only reflect the latest trends but also encapsulate the unique personality of each client.

- ➢ **Confidences Shared in Hushed Tones**. Unveil the hushed tones and confidential exchanges that characterize salon visits. It's a space where residents feel comfortable sharing their deepest desires and life's triumphs and tribulations.

- ➢ **Salon as a Culmination of Culture**. Examine how Manhattan's salons serve as a culmination of diverse cultures, where hairstylists draw inspiration from around the world to create a rich tapestry of styles that celebrate the city's multiculturalism.

As we conclude our exploration of The Salons of Manhattan's Magic, remember that in this city, salons are not just places for grooming, but sanctuaries where dreams and aspirations take shape. It's where residents entrust their locks to skilled artisans who understand the significance of every strand. In the world of The Manhattan Diaries, we've uncovered the stories, the artistry, and the magic that unfolds within Manhattan's salons. So, my darlings, let your hair be your canvas, and let the city's skilled artisans be your guides as you embrace the transformative experience that is the salon culture of Manhattan.

Completed Tasks: Manhattan Magic Activities

Inspirational Quote

HAPPINESS RESIDES NOT IN POSSESSIONS, AND NOT IN GOLD, HAPPINESS DWELLS IN THE SOUL. — Democritus

Action Items: Intentions and Thoughts

Action Items: Intentions and Thoughts

Cocktail Coiffures:
Hairstyles to Sip Martinis In

Manhattan, a city that doesn't just observe—it scrutinizes, right down to the way your hair frames your face as you sip on that martini. In this enigmatic labyrinth of ambition and aspiration, it isn't merely about arriving at that posh cocktail bar; it's about doing so with a hairdo that commands attention, incites whispers, and seals deals—all before the olive is plucked from your glass.

Now imagine: You're swaying down Fifth Avenue, and while your attire might be impeccable, it's the delicate dance of your tresses, catching the city lights, that's the true showstopper. That, darling, is the Manhattan Hair-Tini Twist—an exquisite blend of elegance and effervescence, all wrapped up in those sumptuous locks.

In this tantalizing chapter of The Manhattan Diaries, you'll be whisked away into the world of high-rise hairdos and penthouse ponytails. From the chic chignon that pairs perfectly with a classic cosmopolitan to the boisterous bob that's the soulmate of a spunky spritz, you'll learn the art of matching your mane to your martini.

But, of course, it's not merely about the hair. It's the embodiment of Manhattan's essence, the silent statement you make as you weave through its streets and alleys. It's about moving with purpose, with a twinkle in your eye and a dream tousled into your curls. It's navigating the neon lights and dark corners with equal flair, making every highball a high note.

So, come with me, as we venture into the salons hidden in Manhattan's penthouses and learn from the maestros of mane. After all, in this city, your hair is not just an accessory—it's your anthem. And, honey, with the right coiffure, every cocktail hour is your curtain call. Welcome to The Manhattan Diaries—where your hair's flair is as intoxicating as the city's most exquisite elixirs.

The Manhattan Hair-Tini Twist

Darlings, prepare to be swept away into the enchanting world of The Manhattan Hair-Tini Twist. In this chapter of The Manhattan Diaries, we shall delve into the intricate dance between elegance and effervescence, where your locks become the true showstopper as you navigate the city's streets and cocktail bars. With a martini in hand and your hair as your crown, let's embark on a journey that pairs sumptuous locks with Manhattan's finest elixirs.

➤ **The Allure of the Manhattan Hair-Tini Twist**. Explore the irresistible allure of the Manhattan Hair-Tini Twist, a coiffure that embodies the city's essence—elegance and effervescence combined into sumptuous locks that catch the city lights and command attention.

➤ **High-Rise Hairdos and Penthouse Ponytails**. Discover the world of high-rise hairdos and penthouse ponytails, where chic chignons complement classic cosmopolitans, and boisterous bobs find their soulmate in spunky spritzes. These coiffures are the perfect match for Manhattan's cocktail culture.

➤ **Sip, Swirl, and Sway**. Embrace the concept that in Manhattan, it's not just about sipping martinis; it's about doing so with style and confidence. Your hair becomes a silent statement that mirrors your purpose, ambition, and flair as you weave through the city's neon lights and dark corners.

➤ **Secrets from the Maestros of Mane**. Venture into the hidden salons of Manhattan's penthouses and learn from the maestros of mane—the skilled stylists who craft these captivating coiffures. Discover the techniques and secrets behind the artistry that steals the spotlight during cocktail hours.

➢ **The Seductive Tango of Hair and Martini**. Delve into the art of the seductive tango that unfolds between your hair and your martini glass. Your locks become an extension of the cocktail experience, adding an element of allure and sophistication.

➢ **The Martini as a Muse**. Explore how the classic martini serves as a muse for hairstylists in Manhattan. Its elegance, clarity, and timeless appeal inspire coiffures that mirror its qualities, creating a harmonious blend of taste and style.

➢ **The Sip-and-Sway Lifestyle**. Embrace the sip-and-sway lifestyle, where each sip of your martini is accompanied by a graceful sway of your coiffured mane. It's a dance that elevates every cocktail hour to a memorable performance.

➢ **Hair as a Manhattan Signature**. Examine how in Manhattan, your hair becomes a signature element of your identity. Just as the city has its iconic landmarks, your coiffure becomes a symbol of your presence, style, and aspiration.

➢ **Cocktails and Curls Collide**. Step into the spotlight where cocktails and curls collide, celebrating the intertwining of Manhattan's vibrant nightlife with elegant, flowing hairstyles. From the flirtatious flick of a curl to the subtle swing of layered locks, each hairstyle echoes the rhythm of the city, perfectly paired with a signature cocktail to toast to the night's adventures.

As we conclude our journey into The Manhattan Hair-Tini Twist, remember that in this city, your hair is not just a canvas; it's your anthem, your declaration, and your invitation to the grand stage of Manhattan. With the right coiffure, every cocktail hour becomes your curtain call, an intoxicating moment in the dazzling narrative of your life. Cheers to The Manhattan Diaries, where your hair's flair shines as brightly as the city's most exquisite elixirs.

Completed Tasks: Hair Fini-Twist Activities

_____

_____

_____

_____

_____

_____

_____

_____

_____

_____

_____

_____

_____

_____

_____

_____

_____

_____

_____

_____

_____

_____

_____

_____

_____

_____

_____

_____

Inspirational Quote

EVERY STORY I CREATE, CREATES ME. I WRITE TO CREATE MYSELF. —
Octavia E. Butler

COCKTAIL COIFFURES

Action Items: Intentions and Thoughts

High-Rise Hairdos and Penthouse Ponytails

Darlings, in the glittering realm of Manhattan, where aspiration knows no bounds, even the tresses that cascade down your shoulders aspire to reach new heights. We're about to embark on a glamorous journey into the world of High-Rise Hairdos and Penthouse Ponytails, where your coiffure becomes the crowning glory of your high-society soirees and penthouse parties. With sophistication and style as our guiding lights, let's explore the allure of these hairdos that elevate Manhattan's elegance to new heights.

➢ **The Chic Chignon: A Classic Cosmopolitan Companion**. Delve into the timeless allure of the chic chignon, a hairstyle that perfectly complements the classic cosmopolitan. Its elegance and grace mirror the sophistication of Manhattan's high-rise soirees, making it a favorite choice among the city's elite.

➢ **Bobs and Spritz: The Spunky Duo of the Penthouse Party**. Explore the lively world of bobs and spritz, a dynamic dua that thrives in the atmosphere of penthouse parties. This spirited hairstyle pairs effortlessly with the spunky spritz cocktail, exuding vivacity and energy.

➢ **Elegance Reimagined: Penthouse Ponytails for Grand Galas**. Unveil the grandeur of penthouse ponytails, hairstyles that redefine elegance for Manhattan's grand galas. These sleek and polished ponytails are the epitome of refinement, a perfect match for upscale events and opulent gatherings.

➢ **The High-Rise Hairdo Philosophy**. Examine the underlying philosophy of high-rise hairdos and penthouse ponytails—the belief that your coiffure is not just a complement to your attire but an integral part of your identity. It's a silent proclamation of your refined taste and your aspiration to reach the pinnacle of Manhattan's social scene.

➢ **The Penthouse Ponytail as a Power Move**. Delve into the notion that a penthouse ponytail is more than just a hairstyle; it's a power move. It exudes confidence, control, and a sense of authority, making it a favorite choice for Manhattan's high-achieving women.

➢ **Hair as an Accessory to Luxury**. Explore how high-rise hairdos and penthouse ponytails are considered not just grooming choices but luxurious accessories that complete an upscale look. These coiffures accentuate the opulence and sophistication of Manhattan's elite.

➢ **The Art of the Updo**. Unveil the artistry behind the updo, a key element of high-rise hairdos. Skilled stylists craft intricate updos that exude elegance, making them ideal for Manhattan's exclusive gatherings and high-society events.

➢ **The Confidence Boost**. Examine the undeniable confidence boost that comes with sporting a high-rise hairdo or penthouse ponytail. It's a transformative experience that empowers individuals, giving them the self-assurance to conquer the city's social scene with grace and poise.

As we conclude our exploration of High-Rise Hairdos and Penthouse Ponytails, remember that in this city, your hair isn't just styled; it's sculpted into a work of art. It's a symbol of your desire to ascend to new heights, both literally and figuratively. In the voice of The Manhattan Diaries, we've uncovered the elegance, sophistication, and aspirations that define Manhattan's high-society hairdos. So, darlings, let your hair be your crown as you elevate your presence at penthouse soirees and high-rise galas. In the dazzling narrative of Manhattan's elite, your coiffure is your statement, your signature, and your ticket to the grandest heights of glamour.

Completed Tasks: Hairdos and Ponytails Activities

Inspirational Quote

TODAY I CHOOSE LIFE. EVERY MORNING WHEN I WAKE UP, I CAN CHOOSE JOY, HAPPINESS, NEGATIVITY, PAIN . . . TO FEEL THE FREEDOM THAT COMES FROM BEING ABLE TO CONTINUE TO MAKE MISTAKES AND CHOICES—TODAY I CHOOSE TO FEEL LIFE, NOT TO DENY MY HUMANITY BUT EMBRACE IT. — Kevyn Aucoin

Action Items: Intentions and Thoughts

Hair as a Silent Statement

Darlings, in the captivating tapestry of Manhattan, your hair isn't just an accessory; it's a silent statement—a proclamation of who you are, where you've been, and where you're headed. We're about to embark on a journey into the heart of Hair as a Silent Statement, where every strand is a word, every hairstyle a sentence, and together, they tell the unique story of each Manhattanite. With the allure of the city as our backdrop, let's explore the fascinating world where hair becomes a voice in the narrative of life.

➢ **The Mane Manifesto: A Declaration of Individuality**. Delve into the concept that your hairstyle is your personal manifesto, a declaration of your individuality. Where it's a bold pixie cut, cascading curls, or sleek straight locks, each style reflects a facet of your unique personality.

➢ **Elegance in the Everyday: The Signature Styles of Manhattan**. Explore how Manhattan's residents often cultivate signature styles that become synonymous with their identity. These iconic looks embody elegance and are meticulously maintained to exude timeless grace.

➢ **The Evolution of Expression: Hairstyles Through the Ages**. Unveil the dynamic evolution of hairstyles in Manhattan, where trends come and go, but the power of personal expression through hair remains constant. Each era brings its own unique statement to the city's vibrant tapestry.

➢ **Silent Conversations at the Salon: Secrets Shared in the Chair**. Examine the intimate conversations that take place in Manhattan's salons, where stylists become confidants, and clients share their dreams, aspirations, and stories as their hair is transformed.

➢ **Hair as a Time Capsule**. Delve into the idea that hairstyles are like time capsules, encapsulating the essence of a specific era or moment in one's life. Whether it's a rebellious pixie cut from your youth or elegant updos that mark special occasions, your hair tells a story of where you've been.

➢ **The Role of Color: Shading Personal Narratives**. Explore how hair color becomes a creative palette for self-expression. From bold hues that exude confidence to subtle shades that signify sophistication, the choice of color adds layers to the silent story your hair conveys.

➢ **The Role of Color: Shading Personal Narratives**. Explore how hair color becomes a creative palette for self-expression. From bold hues that exude confidence to subtle shades that signify sophistication, the choice of color adds layers to the silent story your hair conveys.

➢ **Manhattan's Subculture Statement**. Unveil the influence of Manhattan's vibrant subcultures on hairstyles. From punk-inspired cuts to bohemian braids, the city's diverse communities create unique coiffures that stand as statements of belonging and individuality.

As we conclude our exploration of Hair as a Silent Statement, remember that in this city, your hair is not just a canvas; it's a living, breathing testament to your identity, your experiences, and your aspirations. In the world of The Manhattan Diaries, we've uncovered the narratives, the elegance, and the silent conversations that unfold in the realm of Manhattan's hairstyles. So, my darlings, let your hair be your voice in this grand narrative, an ever-changing statement that resonates through the streets, the skyscrapers, and the stories of this extraordinary city.

Completed Tasks: Silent Statement Activities

_____

_____

_____

_____

_____

_____

_____

_____

_____

_____

_____

_____

_____

_____

_____

_____

_____

_____

_____

_____

_____

_____

_____

_____

_____

_____

Inspirational Quote

THE POWER OF IMAGINATION MAKES US INFINITE. — John Muir

COCKTAIL COIFFURES

Action Items: Intentions and Thoughts

The Maestros of Mane

Darlings, in the heart of Manhattan's glamour, where ambition and elegance converge, there exists a hidden realm—a place where the artistry of hair transcends mere grooming and becomes a masterpiece. We're about to embark on a journey into the world of The Maestros of Mane, where skilled stylists transform hair into living sculptures, creating works of art that elevate Manhattan's elite to unparalleled heights of beauty and confidence. With the allure of the city as our backdrop, let's uncover the secrets, the creativity, and the passion that define these gifted artisans.

➢ **Stylists: The Architects of Manhattan's Crowning Glory.** Delve into the world of stylists, where they are not just hairdressers but architects of Manhattan's crowning glory. There artistry goes beyond scissors and combs; it's about sculpting hair into exquisite forms that mirror the personality and aspirations of each client.

➢ **The Salon Sanctuaries.** Explore the sanctuaries that are Manhattan's salons, where stylists and clients engage in a unique dance of creativity and collaboration. These spaces are where visions come to life, where confidences are shared, and where transformations occur.

➢ **Secrets of the Chair: Confidential Conversations.** Uncover the intimate conversations that transpire in the salon chair. As stylists work their magic, clients share their dreams, desires, and stories, creating a bond that goes beyond hair, making the stylist a trusted confidant.

➢ **The Maestro's Signature: Creating Iconic Styles.** Examine the notion that every maestro of mane has a signature touch—a unique ability to craft iconic styles that become synonymous with their name. These styles transcend trends, becoming timeless classics that define an era.

➤ **The Art of Customization**. Delve into the art of customization that defines Manhattan's hairstylists. They don't just follow trends; they curate unique styles that cater to the individual needs and desires of each client, creating bespoke coiffures that stand out in the crowd.

➤ **Innovation in the Chair**. Explore how innovation is a driving force in the salon chair. From cutting-edge techniques to groundbreaking products, Manhattan's stylists are at the forefront of the beauty industry, constantly pushing boundaries to achieve hair perfection.

➤ **From Runway to Real Life**. Unveil the seamless transition from runway glamour to everyday elegance. Manhattan's stylists have the uncanny ability to translate high-fashion looks into wearable, yet striking, styles that allow clients to effortlessly embody Manhattan's cosmopolitan chic.

➤ **The Maestros' Muse**. Examine the diverse sources of inspiration that fuel the creativity of Manhattan's hairstylists. From art and architecture to the city's vibrant subcultures, these maestros draw from a rich tapestry of influences to craft hair masterpieces that capture the essence of the metropolis.

As we conclude our journey into The Maestros of Mane, remember that in this city, your hairstylist is not just a professional; they are an artist, a confidant, and as collaborators in the masterpiece that is your hair. In the world of The Manhattan Diaries, we've unveiled the creativity, the secrets, and the personal connections that define the world of Manhattan's hairstylists. So, darlings, let your hair be your canvas, and let the maestros of mane be your guides as you embrace the transformative experience that is the salon culture of Manhattan. In the grand narrative of life, your coiffure is your statement, your masterpiece, and your declaration of beauty and confidence.

Completed Tasks: Hair Maestros Activities

Action Items: Intentions and Thoughts

Action Items: Intentions and Thoughts

The Park Avenue Ponytail:
A Twist on the Classic Updo

Manhattan, a city that doesn't just observe—it delves deep, noticing the tiniest shift in a hairstyle, the subtlest twirl of an updo. It's a city that understands that ambition isn't just about reaching the top, but how you wear your crown, especially when that crown is a chic twist on a classic. In these streets, it's not just about reaching that swanky rooftop soiree, it's about ensuring your hairstyle holds its own amidst the city's towering giants.

Now imagine: You're dancing down Fifth Avenue, the light catching every intricacy of that Park Avenue Ponytail, causing a ripple of admiration. It's not the shimmer of your jewelry or the sway of your dress that has them entranced—it's that twist, that audacious elevation of a classic that speaks of heritage yet screams modernity. That, darling, is the Manhattan Hair Play—a game where the stakes are as high as the city's skyscrapers.

In this sizzling chapter of The Manhattan Diaries, we'll dive deep into the world of the Park Avenue Ponytail. From the elegantly teased crown to the ribbon-wrapped end, from the loose tendril that whispers secrets to the strong twist that shouts success, you'll unravel the enigma of this iconic updo.

But it's more than hair—it's a statement. It's a nod to Manhattan's grandeur and a wink to its playful side. It's about moving in sync with the city's rhythm, letting your hair narrate tales of soirees and sunrises, of dreams dreamed in penthouses and on park benches.

So, join me, as we ascend to the penthouse salons, seeking the secrets of this metropolitan mane magic. In Manhattan, your hairstyle isn't just a part of you—it's a part of the city's ever-evolving tale. And when you sport the Park Avenue Ponytail, you're not just turning heads; you're turning pages in the city's chronicles. Welcome to The Manhattan Diaries—where your hair tells tales as timeless as the city's horizon.

The Park Avenue Ponytail Unveiled

Darlings, in the thrilling tapestry of Manhattan's cosmopolitan streets, we often find ourselves in a whirlwind of style and sophistication. It's a city that demands attention to detail, where even the slightest shift in a hairstyle is noticed and appreciated. Today, we're embarking on a journey to unveil the mesmerizing Park Avenue Ponytail, a twist on the classic updo that has taken the city by storm. With its audacious elevation of tradition and its modern allure, this hairstyle is more than just a choice—it's a statement. Join me as we explore the intricacies of The Park Avenue Ponytail Unveiled, where style meets ambition, and classic meets contemporary.

> ➤ **A Reimagined Classic Updo: Tradition Meets Modernity.** In the world of the Park Avenue Ponytail, we discover a reimagined classic updo, where tradition and modernity coexist in perfect harmony. It's a hairstyle that captures the essence of Manhattan, reflecting the city's dynamic spirit.

> ➤ **Elegance in the Teased Crown: The Regal Touch.** The elegance of the Park Avenue Ponytail lies in its intricately teased crown. This element adds a touch of regal charm to the modern look, setting it apart and captivating those who appreciate sophistication in its finest form.

> ➤ **Playful Ribbon-Wrapped End: Nod to Individuality.** Adding a playful twist to the traditional updo, the ribbon-wrapped end is a nod to individuality and Manhattan's vibrant, ever-evolving spirit. It serves as a symbol of modernity, infusing the hairstyle with contemporary flair.

> ➤ **Dynamic Character: Whispers of Elegance and Shouts of Ambition.** The Park Avenue Ponytail is a dynamic character, where loose tendrils whisper secrets of elegance and success, while the strong twist shouts ambition and modernity. This hairstyle

encapsulates the diverse narratives of Manhattan, making it a favorite choice among the city's elite.

- ➤ **Crafting the Perfect Ponytail: Artistry Meets Precision**. Dive into the meticulous process of crafting the perfect Park Avenue Ponytail. It's a delicate balance of artistry and precision, where skilled hands transform every strand into a work of elegance.

- ➤ **Versatility Beyond the Uptown Streets: The Ponytail's Adaptability**. Beyond the uptown streets of Manhattan, it's a hairstyle that effortlessly transitions from formal events to casual outings, showcasing its versatility and timeless appeal.

- ➤ **Sleek Lines, Bold Statement: The Silhouette of Power**. The sleek lines of the Park Avenue Ponytail not only complement the contours of the face but also project a bold statement of power and control. This silhouette makes it a staple for those who wish to command presence in both boardrooms and at social galas, embodying the quintessential New York City power dressing.

- ➤ **Cultural Icon: The City's Pulse**. More than a hairstyle, the Park Avenue Ponytail is a symbol of Manhattan's fast-paced life and relentless pursuit of excellence, mirroring the city's cultural pulse.

As we conclude our journey through The Park Avenue Ponytail Unveiled, remember that in Manhattan, your hairstyle isn't just an accessory; it's a part of your personal narrative. The Park Avenue Ponytail embodies the city's essence, where classic beauty meets contemporary ambition. In the world of The Manhattan Diaries, we've explored the audacious elevation of tradition and the captivating allure of modernity in this iconic hairstyle. So, darlings, embrace the sophistication, style, and timeless elegance of the Park Avenue Ponytail as you navigate the dazzling streets of Manhattan, leaving an indelible mark in the city's narrative of glamour and ambition.

Completed Tasks: Reimagined Ponytail Activities

_____
_____
_____
_____
_____
_____
_____
_____
_____
_____
_____
_____
_____
_____
_____
_____
_____
_____
_____
_____
_____
_____
_____
_____
_____
_____

Inspirational Quote

COUNTLESS AS THE SANDS OF THE SEA ARE HUMAN PASSIONS. — Nikolai Gogol

Action Items: Intentions and Thoughts

The Anatomy of Elegance

Darlings, in the glittering world of Manhattan's high society, elegance is not merely a trait—it's an art form. It's the secret to turning heads and leaving an indelible mark. Today, we delve into The Anatomy of Elegance, where we dissect the components that transform a look into a Manhattan masterpiece. Join me on this journey, where style, grace, and sophistication intertwine to create an enchanting narrative.

- ➢ **The First Impression: The Power of a Well-Structured Ensemble**. Explore the significance of a well-structured ensemble as the cornerstone of elegance. It's the first impression that sets the stage for the rest of the ensemble, defining the aura of sophistication that follows.

- ➢ **The Art of Tailoring: A Flawless Fit**. Delve into the importance of tailoring, where every stitch and seam is meticulously crafted to ensure a flawless fit. It's the foundation upon which elegance is built, ensuring that every garment drapes in harmony with the body.

- ➢ **The Timeless Palette: Neutral Tones and Classic Hues**. Discuss the timeless palette of neutral tones and classic hues that exude sophistication. These colors form the canvas upon which elegance is painted, allowing the wearer to shine without distraction.

- ➢ **Accessories: Subtle Statements**. Explore how accessories play a vital role in the anatomy of elegance. They are not loud or ostentatious but rather subtle statements that enhance the overall allure, drawing attention to exquisite details.

- ➢ **The Poise Factor: Graceful Movement and Confidence**. Highlight the importance of poise, where graceful movement and confidence elevate elegance to its pinnacle. It's not just about what you wear, but how you carry yourself that leaves a lasting impression.

➢ **The Symphony of Fabrics: Luxurious Textures and Timeless Fabrics**. Elegance is also woven into the very fabric of your ensemble. Luxurious textures and timeless fabrics, such as silk, cashmere, the fine wool, create a tactile symphony that complements the visual allure. The sensation of these materials against your skin adds depth to the elegance you exude.

➢ **The Elegance of Hair: A Crowning Glory**. In Manhattan's elegance, hair is key. A chic bun or flowing waves can perfect an outfit, reflecting personal style and city sophistication.

➢ **Personal Expression: The Art of Accessorizing with Grace**. Beyond their visual appeal, accessories serve as expressions of your individuality. The choice of a statement necklace, a delicate brooch, or a vintage watch tells a story and adds a touch of your unique charm to the ensemble. Accessorizing with grace is an art, and it's the hallmark of a true Manhattan sophisticate.

➢ **Elegance Beyond Attire: Etiquette and Graciousness**. Elegance extends beyond clothing—it's a way of conducting oneself. Etiquette and graciousness, the elegant codes of behavior, define the true Manhattan elite. Politeness, kindness, and an understanding of social graces complete the portrait of a person truly embodying elegance.

As we conclude our exploration of The Anatomy of Elegance, remember that in Manhattan, elegance is not a fleeting trend; it's a way of life. It's the careful selection of elements that come together to create a masterpiece—a visual symphony that resonates with style, grace, and sophistication. In the world of The Manhattan Diaries, we've unveiled the secrets of timeless elegance, and I encourage you, my darlings, to embrace these components in your own journey through the dazzling streets of Manhattan. Elegance isn't just a trait; it's a statement, narrative, and testament.

Completed Tasks: Turning Heads Activities

_____
_____
_____
_____
_____
_____
_____
_____
_____
_____
_____
_____
_____
_____
_____
_____
_____
_____
_____
_____
_____
_____
_____
_____
_____
_____

Inspirational Quote

HAPPINESS IS NOT SOMETHING YOU POSTPONE FOR THE FUTURE; IT IS SOMETHING YOU DESIGN FOR THE PRESENT. — Jim Rohn

Action Items: Intentions and Thoughts

Manhattan's Hair Play

Manhattan's Hair Play epitomizes the high stakes of style in a city that never sleeps. This unique concept isn't just about flaunting a hairstyle; it's a dynamic narrative of one's journey through the iconic landscapes and times of Manhattan. Each twist and curl is a silent testament to the soirees attended and the dreams chased from sunrises on penthouse terraces to quiet moments on park benches. Here, your hairstyle does more than complement your outfit—it narrates your place in the city's ongoing saga.

➢ **Skyline Silhouettes.** Capture the essence of Manhattan's skyline with hairstyles that mimic the city's architectural lines—sharp bobs or soft layers that reflect modern art forms, celebrating the city's structural beauty.

➢ **Twilight Tresses.** Opt for styles that shimmer under the city lights with rich colors and highlights perfect for glamorous evenings. From sparkling updos to wavy locks, these styles make every night out an event.

➢ **Dawn Designs.** Inspired by the peaceful, early morning hours in Central Park, these hairstyles are all about soft, effortless elegance. Think loose, comfortable buns wrapped in silk scarves or gentle waves that catch the first light of day. Dawn designs are perfect for those serene moments of solitude or early morning coffee runs, offering a look that's as refreshing as the morning dew.

➢ **Cocktail Curls.** Perfect for the social butterfly, cocktail curls are lush, vibrant, and full of life, designed to keep heads turning through hours of nightlife and networking. These curls are crafted to be resilient and radiant, bouncing back with every laugh and turn. Whether it's tight, defined curls or big, bold waves, each lock is a toast to the city's dynamic social scene.

➢ **Rooftop Ripples**. Casual yet chic, rooftop ripples are inspired by the laid-back luxury of Manhattan's rooftop gatherings. These wavy hairstyles flow with ease, offering a relaxed yet polished look that's ideal for a sunny afternoon or a casual evening out. The waves are styled to look effortlessly put together, embodying the spirit of a city that's both lively and luxurious.

➢ **Boardroom Braids**. Sleek, polished braids that signify power and precision, ideal for conquering negotiations and presentations. These aren't just any braids; they're meticulously crafted to convey confidence and control.

➢ **Penthouse Ponytails**. Symbolizing ambition and clarity, the penthouse ponytail is all about elevating a simple style to new heights. This isn't just a ponytail; it's a statement of intent, styled high on the head with a smooth, sleek finish that commands respect and admiration from every angle. It's the perfect complement to a view from the top, reflecting the wearer's lofty aspirations.

➢ **Park Bench Waves**. Soft and inviting, park bench waves capture the reflective, more introspective side of Manhattan life. These waves are loose and flowing, suggesting a relaxed confidence and a deep connection to the city's cultural pulse. They're the kind of style that's perfect for a leisurely day spent in one of the city's many parks, offering both comfort and a touch of elegance.

As the curtain falls on Manhattan's Hair Play, remember that each style is more than just a fashion statement—it's a piece of the narrative that is New York. Whether you're stepping out onto Fifth Avenue or attending an exclusive gala, your hair tells a story of ambition, beauty, and the relentless pursuit of dreams in the city that never sleeps. Embrace your role in The Manhattan Diaries, where every hairstyle is a chapter of your unique urban tale.

Completed Tasks: Hair Play Activities

Inspirational Quote

BE BRAVE ENOUGH TO LIVE LIFE CREATIVELY. THE CREATIVE PLACE WHERE NO ONE ELSE HAS EVER BEEN. — Alan Alda

THE PARK AVENUE PONYTAIL

Action Items: Intentions and Thoughts

81

Turning Heads and Pages

In the glittering realm of Manhattan, where each street corner whispers tales of ambition and every glance conceals secrets, there exists a seductive dance between two worlds: fashion and literature. It's a realm where the narratives of style and the written world intertwine, creating a symphony of fascination that transcends the ordinary. Join me, dear readers, as we step into this enchanting chapter of Turning Heads and Pages. Here, in the heart of Manhattan, we'll explore how the city's elite have mastered the art of transforming fashion into literature, where attire becomes the pages of their life stories, and where iconic styles penned by fashion legends through the decades continue to captivate our imaginations.

➢ **The Literary Runway: Fashion as a Storyteller**. On the illustrious literary runway of Manhattan, fashion emerges as a masterful storyteller. In the choices of attire, one can uncover tales of self-expression, identity, and aspirations. Each ensemble becomes a chapter in the narrative of an individual's life, revealing hints of their character and the adventures they dare to embark upon.

➢ **Fashion Icons as Protagonists: Iconic Styles Through the Decades**. Fashion icons, those legendary figures who grace the pages of history, are the veritable protagonists of their own sagas. Their styles evolve, creating a visual chronicle of the times. Journey through the decades, from the timeless elegance of Audrey Hepburn to the sensuality of Marilyn Monroe and the fearless creativity of Lady Gaga, exploring how they've penned unforgettable chapters in the story of fashion.

➢ **The Couturier as Author: Creating Fashion as Literature**. Within the ateliers of Manhattan, the couturier is an author in their own right. They craft garments that tell tales of innovation, rebellion, and societal shifts. Delve into the narratives woven by legendary designers such as Coco Chanel and Alexander McQueen, who have authored chapters in the fashion storybook, each with its own profound impact on the world of style.

- ➤ **Literature's Influence on Fashion: The Power of the Written Word**. Literature possesses a transformative power, inspiring designers to draw from classic novels, poems, and literary movements. Witness how the written word metamorphoses into wearable art, materializing in collections inspired by the timeless works of Jane Austen, the roaring decadence of F. Scott Fitzgerald, and the timeless verses of Shakespeare, creating a harmonious fusion of the literary and sartorial worlds.

- ➤ **The Language of Texture: Fabric as Prose and Poetry**. In the world of fashion and literature, fabric becomes the language of texture, akin to the prose and poetry of an exquisite novel. Explore how choices in textiles, from the soft caress of silk to the structured elegance of tweed, create tactile narratives that enhance the storytelling of attire.

- ➤ **Style as a Memoir: Fashion Through Life Stages**. Style evolves through life's chapters, much like the chapters of a memoir. Discover how individuals use fashion to reflect their personal growth and transformation, embracing new narratives with each phase of life.

As we conclude our mesmerizing exploration of Turning Heads and Pages, remember that in the city that never sleeps, fashion and literature are more than just elements of life—they are life itself. They narrate the dynamic tales of self-expression and cultural evolution, where style becomes literature and literature becomes style. Embrace this enchanting fusion as you navigate the captivating streets of Manhattan, turning heads and pages in the grand story of your own Manhattan Chronicles.

Completed Tasks: Turning Heads Activities

_____
_____
_____
_____
_____
_____
_____
_____
_____
_____
_____
_____
_____
_____
_____
_____
_____
_____
_____
_____
_____
_____
_____
_____
_____
_____

Inspirational Quote

IF YOU ARE POSITIVE, YOU'LL SEE OPPORTUNITIES INSTEAD OF OBSTACLES. — Widad Akrawi

Action Items: Intentions and Thoughts

Action Items: Intentions and Thoughts

Brunching and Braiding:
Uptown Styles for Lazy Sundays

Manhattan, a city that doesn't merely glimpse—it becomes enamored, noticing the fine intricacies of every braid that tumbles down the shoulders of the city's elite. Here, it's clear that ambition isn't solely reserved for boardrooms; it manifests in the brunch spots where mimosas meet meticulous hairstyles. Because in this city, a laid-back Sunday still deserves an updo with flair.

Now picture this: You're sauntering down Fifth Avenue, the sun reflecting off penthouse windows, casting a golden hue on you. And while many might be entranced by the glint of your sunglasses, it's the twist and turn of your braids, woven tales of luxury and leisure, that really capture their gaze. That, my dear, is the Manhattan Hair Story—a narrative spun with every strand, embodying chic relaxation.

In this tantalizing chapter of The Manhattan Diaries, you'll venture into the sanctum of Sunday styles, where brunching isn't just a meal, it's an event. From the elegant waterfall braid to the boho fishtail, from the relaxed French plait to the intricate crown braid, you'll learn how to wear your story, sip by sip, braid by braid.

Yet, it's not merely about hair—it's a lifestyle. It's understanding that in Manhattan, even on a lazy Sunday, you move to the city's slow yet purposeful beat, with each braid representing tales of past adventures and those yet to come.

So, let's journey together, weaving between the city's iconic brunch spots and the salons that prep you for them. In Manhattan, your hairstyle isn't an afterthought—it's a conversation starter. As you delicately fork that avocado toast and tip your glass, remember: your braid isn't just a style; it's an anthem. Welcome to The Manhattan Diaries—where every twist in your hair is a testament to Manhattan's captivating charm.

Brunching and Braiding

In the heart of Manhattan, where every moment is an opportunity to make a statement, we've delved into the captivating world of Brunching and Braiding. As you savor that final bite of avocado toast and raise your glass for one last toast, remember that every twist in your braid is a testament to this city's charm. In The Manhattan Diaries, your hair tells a tale of leisure and luxury, woven into the vibrant fabric of the city. May your braids continue to captivate, adding a touch of chic relaxation to the bustling streets of Manhattan.

> ➢ **Brunching and Braiding: Uptown Styles for Lazy Sundays**. In the bustling heart of Manhattan, where ambition and leisure entwine like old lovers, we step into a chapter that celebrates the art of brunching and braiding. Here, amidst the city's elite, explore how even on a lazy Sunday, Manhattanites continue to craft narratives of chic relaxation and sophisticated style.

> ➢ **The Brunch Culture: A Sunday Social Soiree**. Brunch in Manhattan isn't just a meal; it's cultural phenomenon. Dive into the world of brunch culture, where mimosas flow like conversation and every bite becomes an indulgent moment. It's a gathering, a lifestyle, and an art form all rolled into one.

> ➢ **Braids: The Literary Strands of Manhattan Hair**. Braids take on a starring role in the Manhattan hair story, becoming the literary strands that weave tales of luxury and leisure. Explore the artistry behind the elegant waterfall braid, the boho fishtail, the relaxed French plait, and the intricate crown braid. Each braid tells its own story, etching its narrative in the Manhattan skyline.

> ➢ **Sunday Serenity: The Slow Luxury of Manhattan**. Sundays in Manhattan embrace a unique blend of serenity and sophistication. Discover how even on a leisurely Sunday, the city's residents move

to a slow yet purposeful beat, with each braid symbolizing tales of past adventures and dreams yet to be fulfilled.

➤ **The Connection: Brunch Spots and Salons**. Join us on a journey as we navigate between Manhattan's iconic brunch spots and the sanctuaries of style—the salons that prepare you for leisurely gatherings. In this city, your hairstyle isn't just an accessory; it's a conversation starter, an emblem of your captivating charm.

➤ **The Braided Brunch Palette: Adorning Hairstyles with Floral Flourishes**. Explore the enchanting world of floral adornments for braids. From delicate blossoms to vibrant blooms, incorporating flowers into your braided styles adds an extra layer of elegance and a touch of whimsy, turning your hair into a canvas of botanical beauty.

➤ **Sunday Rituals: The Art of Self-Care and Relaxation**. Sundays in Manhattan are not just about brunch; they are also about self-care and relaxation. Learn how to curate your own Sunday rituals, from indulgent spa treatments to tranquil meditation.

➤ **A Braided Anthem: Captivating Charm on Lazy Sundays**. As we conclude our exploration of Brunching and Braiding, remember that in the grand narrative of The Manhattan Diaries, every twist and turn in your braid is a testament to this city's magnetic allure. So, embrace leisurely Sundays, relish the art of braiding, and let Manhattan's rhythmic heartbeat guide you through each twist and turn of your own Manhattan Hair Story.

As we embark on this enchanting journey through Brunching and Braiding, remember that in Manhattan, every twist of your braid tells a story—a testament to the city's magnetic allure. So, sip that mimosa, relish your avocado toast, and let your braid be your anthem in this exhilarating chapter of The Manhattan Diaries.

Completed Tasks: Brunching and Braiding Activities

Inspirational Quote

NOTHING MAKES ONE FEEL SO STRONG AS A CALL FOR HELP. — Pope Paul VI

Action Items: Intentions and Thoughts

Brunch: The Social Soiree of Sunday

In the enchanting realm of Manhattan, where every moment is an opportunity to mingle, we step into the mesmerizing chapter of Brunch: The Social Soiree of Sunday. Here, in the heart of the city that never sleeps, we'll explore how Sunday brunch isn't just a meal—it's a lavish affair, a social spectacle, and an art form that transcends the ordinary.

➤ **A Midday Celebration: Brunch as an Experience**. Brunch in Manhattan is more than just sustenance; it's an extravagant experience. Dive into the world of midday celebrations, where mimosas flow like conversations, and every dish becomes a canvas for culinary artistry. Discover how brunch is an ode to leisure and camaraderie, a moment to savor life's pleasures.

➤ **The Gathering of Elite Tastemakers: Manhattan's Brunch Scene**. Manhattan's brunch scene is a gathering of elite tastemakers, where the city's most discerning residents come together to see and be seen. Explore the hottest brunch spots, from chic rooftop terraces to cozy neighborhood bistros, and witness how brunch becomes a social soiree where connections are forged and stories are shared.

➤ **Fashion as Brunch Attire: Dressing for the Occasion**. Dressing for brunch is an art form in itself. Learn how Manhattanites embrace fashion as a vital component of the brunch experience. From elegant daytime ensembles to casual chic attire, discover the style secrets that make brunch outfits a statement of sophistication and individuality.

➤ **Toast to Friendship: The Power of Mimosa-Fueled Conversations**. Raise your glass to friendship as we delve into the power of mimosa-fueled conversations. Brunch is not just about food and drink; it's about connecting with friends, both old and new. Witness how the effervescence of champagne-infused discussions turns brunch into a social soiree filled with laughter, anecdotes, and shared dreams.

➢ **A Sunday Ritual: Brunch as a Manhattan Tradition**. Brunch is more than a meal; it's a Manhattan tradition. Discover how even in the city's fast-paced rhythm, Sundays offer a moment of respite, a chance to indulge in the leisurely pleasure of brunch. It's a ritual that encapsulates the essence of Manhattan living.

➢ **The Art of Reservation: Brunch Planning as an Affair**. Uncover the intricate dance of making brunch reservations in Manhattan. Learn the delicate balance between securing a coveted spot at the trendiest eateries and ensuring a relaxed, unhurried dining experience with friends.

➢ **The Rise of the Brunch Cocktail: Mixology Magic at Midday**. Explore the evolution of brunch cocktails beyond the classic mimosa. From innovative Bloody Mary variations to brunch-themed craft cocktails, discover how mixologists in Manhattan have elevated midday libations to an art, perfectly complementing the experience.

➢ **Brunch Etiquette: Navigating the Social Labyrinth**. Delve into the unwritten rules and nuances of brunch etiquette in Manhattan. From the timing of reservations to the delicate balance of conversation and culinary enjoyment, grasp the art of seamlessly navigating the social labyrinth of a Manhattan brunch gathering.

As we conclude our exploration of Brunch: The Social Soiree of Sunday, remember that in this city of dreams, brunch isn't just a culinary delight; it's a celebration of life, style, and connection. So, raise your mimosa-filled glass to the enchanting moments, the delectable dishes, and the vibrant conversations that make brunch a social soiree like no other. Here in The Manhattan Diaries, every brunch is a story waiting to unfold, and every bite is a taste of the city's allure.

Completed Tasks: Sunday Social Soirees Activities

BRUNCHING AND BRAIDING

Action Items: Intentions and Thoughts

Braids as Stories: The Manhattan Hair Tale

In the heart of Manhattan, where every detail is scrutinized and every style speaks volumes, we step into the captivating world of Braids as Stories: The Manhattan Hair Tale. Here, amidst the city's pulsating rhythm, we'll explore how braids aren't merely hairstyles; they are tales woven with the threads of ambition, elegance, and individuality.

> ➢ **Elegant Waterfall Braids: Cascading Narratives of Grace**. The elegant waterfall braid is more than just a hairstyle; it's a narrative of grace. Discover the artistry behind this timeless braid, where delicate strands cascade like a story's plot, creating an ethereal aura that captures the essence of sophistication.

> ➢ **Boho Fishtail Braids: Tales of Carefree Bohemian Spirit**. Boho fishtail braids are a reflection of carefree, bohemian spirit. Dive into the world of these intricate yet playful braids, where each strand tells a story of artistic freedom and the desire to embrace life's adventures with a hint of whimsy.

> ➢ **Relaxed French Plaits: Stories of Effortless Chic**. Relaxed French plaits are the embodiment of effortless chic. Explore the allure of these casually elegant braids, where every twist and turn whispers tales of leisurely strolls through Manhattan's hidden gems, exuding a natural charm that's impossible to resist.

> ➢ **Intricate Crown Braids: Regal Narratives of Confidence**. Delve into the world of these captivating braids, where each twist and turn forms a metaphorical crown, declaring the wearer's authority and self-assuredness in the grand tapestry of Manhattan life.

> ➢ **The Braided Legacy: An Ode to Cultural Diversity**. Braids in Manhattan celebrate cultural diversity. Discover how different braid

styles pay homage to various traditions and backgrounds, creating a rich tapestry of narratives that reflect the city's multicultural essence.

➢ **Runway to Sidewalk: Braids as Everyday Runway Statements**. From fashion runways to the city sidewalks, braids have transcended boundaries. Explore how Manhattanites effortlessly incorporate runway-inspired braid styles into their everyday lives, turning the bustling streets into a runway of individuality and style.

➢ **The Braid Artistry: Salons as Storytelling Sanctuaries**. Salons in Manhattan are more than just places for hairstyling; they are storytelling sanctuaries. Journey into the world of salon artistry, where expert braiders bring the narratives to life, crafting each braid as a work of art that resonates with the wearer's unique story.

➢ **Sculptural Updo Braids: Architectural Expressions of Style**. Embrace the creativity of sculptural updo braids that reflect Manhattan's architectural elegance. These braids are not just hairdos; they are structural masterpieces that echo the city's iconic buildings, showcasing an artistic interpretation of urban aesthetics through the artful intertwining of hair.

➢ **Nightlife Twisted Braids: Pulse of the City**. Explore the energetic nightlife of Manhattan with twisted braids that reflect the city's dynamic after-dark vibes. These braids symbolize the constant motion and rhythm of Manhattan's lively evenings.

As we conclude our exploration of Braids as Stories: The Manhattan Hair Tale, remember that in this city, even the simplest braid becomes a part of the Manhattan Hair Tapestry—a living, breathing narrative that captures the spirit of ambition, individuality, and timeless elegance. Every braid is a chapter, every twist is a sentence, and every strand is a word in the story of Manhattan's captivating charm. Embrace the allure of braids as storytellers, and let your hair narrate your own Manhattan tale.

Completed Tasks: Braids and Hair Tales Activities

_____
_____
_____
_____
_____
_____
_____
_____
_____
_____
_____
_____
_____
_____
_____
_____
_____
_____
_____
_____
_____
_____
_____
_____
_____
_____

Inspirational Quote

IT IS OFTEN SAID THAT BEFORE YOU DIE YOUR LIFE PASSES BEFORE YOUR EYES. IT IS IN FACT TRUE. IT'S CALLED LIVING. — Terry Pratchett

Action Items: Intentions and Thoughts

Sunday Serenity: Embracing Slow Luxury

In the heart of Manhattan, where every moment is a whirlwind of ambition and exhilaration, we step into the serene chapter of Sunday Serenity: Embracing Slow Luxury. Here, amidst the city's relentless pace, we'll uncover the art of slowing down on Sundays—an oasis of calm and indulgence in the bustling urban landscape.

> ➤ **A Leisurely Start: Crafting the Perfect Morning Ritual**. Sunday mornings in Manhattan are reserved for crafting the perfect morning ritual. Dive into the art of leisurely starts, from savoring a decadent breakfast in bed to enjoying a quiet moment with a cup of artisanal coffee. It's a deliberate choice to embrace the luxury of unhurried moments.

> ➤ **Unwinding in Style: The Manhattan Bath Experience**. The Manhattan bath experience is a ritual of relaxation and style. Explore the world of opulent baths adorned with scented candles, exquisite bath oils, and plush robes. It's a sensorial journey that elevates bathing to an art form, offering a respite from the city's constant motion.

> ➤ **The Culinary Odyssey: Dining as an Exploration**. Sunday dining in Manhattan is an exploration of culinary delights. Delve into the world of brunches at chic bistros and sumptuous tasting menus at fine dining establishments. It's a gastronomic journey that allows Manhattanites to savor flavors from around the world without leaving the city's embrace.

> ➤ **Reconnecting with Manhattan's Hidden Gems: Strolls with Purpose**. Rediscover Manhattan's hidden gems through purposeful strolls. Learn how leisurely walks through iconic neighborhoods and serene parks offer a chance to reconnect with the city's essence and uncover new facets of its charm.

➤ **The Power of Mindfulness: Meditative Moments in the City**. Discover how Manhattanites incorporate mindfulness into their Sunday routines. Explore the art of meditation, yoga, or simply taking a few minutes to pause and breathe amidst the city's vibrant chaos, finding inner peace and clarity.

➤ **Artistic Escapes: Museums and Galleries as Sunday Sanctuaries**. Museums and galleries in Manhattan serve as Sunday sanctuaries for art enthusiasts. Learn how leisurely visits to these cultural havens allow residents to immerse themselves in creativity and inspiration, finding solace in the masterpieces that grace the city's walls.

➤ **The Gift of Time: Personal Reflection and Gratitude**. Embrace the gift of time for personal reflection and gratitude on Sundays. Explore how Manhattanites use this day to journal, express gratitude, and set intentions for the week ahead, fostering a sense of inner balance and purpose in the midst of their bustling lives.

➤ **Literary Lounging: Book Cafes and Quiet Corners**. Discover the charm of Manhattan's book cafes and quiet corners where literary lovers gather to unwind. Sundays are perfect for losing yourself in a good book within the cozy confines of a cafe, combining the pleasures of coffee and captivating reads.

As we conclude our exploration of Sunday Serenity: Embracing Slow Luxury, remember that in this city of boundless ambition, embracing slow luxury on Sundays is a lifestyle choice. It's a conscious decision to savor the present, nurture the soul, and find balance amidst the whirlwind of Manhattan life. Each unhurried moment becomes a precious gem in the tapestry of a Manhattanite's journey.

Completed Tasks: Calm and Indulgence Activities

_____

_____

_____

_____

_____

_____

_____

_____

_____

_____

_____

_____

_____

_____

_____

_____

_____

_____

_____

_____

_____

_____

_____

_____

_____

_____

_____

_____

_____

_____

Inspirational Quote

LIFE IS THE ART OF DRAWING SUFFICIENT CONCLUSIONS FROM INSUFFICIENT PREMISES. — Samuel Butler

Action Items: Intentions and Thoughts

The Brunch and Braid Connection: Salons and Sanctums

In the heart of Manhattan, where every detail is meticulously curated and every brunch is an event, we step into the intriguing chapter of The Brunch Braid Connection: Salons and Sanctums. Here, amidst the city's ceaseless buzz, we'll uncover the enthralling relationship between Sunday brunch and the sanctuaries where Manhattanites transform their hair into works of art.

➢ **Salons as Pre-Brunch Sanctums: The Art of Hair Transformation**. Salons in Manhattan become pre-brunch sanctums, where the art of hair transformation unfolds. Discover how expert stylists bring visions to life, crafting braids and updos that elevate the brunch experience, making each strand a statement of elegance and individuality.

➢ **Braid Bar Experiences: Sipping and Styling in Harmony**. Braid bars in Manhattan redefine the brunch experience. Explore how these stylish establishments offer the perfect fusion of sipping cocktails and having your hair styled. It's an immersive experience where hairstyling becomes an integral part of the brunch ritual.

➢ **The Ritual of Salon Conversation: Bonding Over Beauty**. Salon visits in Manhattan are not just about beauty; they are about bonding. Delve into the world of salon conversation, where Manhattanites share stories, tips, and life updates with fellow patrons and stylists, turning hair appointments into social soirees.

➢ **The Seamless Transition: From Salon Chair to Brunch Table**. Experience the seamless transition from salon chair to brunch table. Learn how Manhattanites effortlessly transition from their salon appointments to the city's chic brunch spots, where their perfectly styled hair becomes the centerpiece of admiration and conversation.

➢ **Salon Inspiration: Brunch-Themed Hairstyles**. Discover how Manhattan salons draw inspiration from brunch themes to create unique and playful hairstyles. From mimosa-infused hair colors to avocado toast-inspired braids, explore the creative fusion of culinary trends and hairstyling.

➢ **Braids as Conversation Starters: Brunching with Confidence**. Braids in Manhattan serve as conversation starters during brunch gatherings. Learn how individuals proudly showcase their intricately styled hair, sparking discussions on hairstyling trends, salons, and the city's vibrant culture.

➢ **The Art of Morning Appointments: Brunch Preparation Rituals**. Explore how Manhattanites strategically schedule their hair transformations to ensure they are brunch-ready, making the transition from salon to table a seamless affair.

➢ **Salon Sanctums as Style Museums: Showcasing Trends and Individuality**. Salons in Manhattan double as style museums, showcasing the latest trends and celebrating individuality. Dive into the world of salon decor and ambiance, where artistry and personal expression merge, creating an environment where clients feel inspired and celebrated.

As we conclude our exploration of Sunday Serenity: Embracing Slow Luxury, remember that in this city of boundless ambition, embracing slow luxury on Sundays is a lifestyle choice. It's a conscious decision to savor the present, nurture the soul, and find balance amidst the whirlwind of Manhattan life. Each unhurried moment becomes a precious gem in the tapestry of a Manhattanite's journey.

Completed Tasks: Salons and Sanctums Activities

Inspirational Quote

TRY TO BE LIKE THE TURTLE—AT EASE IN YOUR OWN SHELL. — Bill Copeland

Action Items: Intentions and Thoughts

Action Items: Intentions and Thoughts

Met Gala Mystique:
The Art of Red Carpet Ready Tresses

Manhattan, a city that doesn't simply witness—it is captivated. Each silhouette under its shimmering lights tells a story of aspiration, passion, and the unyielding allure of dreams realized. And in this metropolis of limitless horizons, the destination isn't the only story; the narrative unfolds in how you present yourself while traversing the journey—with grace, allure, and that indefinable New York swank.

Envision this: You're gracefully navigating Fifth Avenue, a sapphire evening gown flowing behind, but what truly turns heads isn't the designer label or the twinkle of your diamond earrings. It's the cascade of meticulously coiffed tresses, shimmering under city lights. That darling, is the Manhattan Hair Elegance—a symphony of locks that exude authority, beauty, and an edge of unexpected drama.

In this intoxicating chapter of The Manhattan Diaries, we delve into the craft of creating the most enchanting hairstyles fit for an evening where the world watches—The Met Gala. From the opulent volume of old Hollywood waves to avant-garde updos that challenge gravity, you'll understand the mastery behind each hair art piece that graces the grand staircase of the Met.

Yet, it transcends the mere strands on one's head. It's about synchronizing with Manhattan's pulsating energy, styling with an underlying story, a vision, a reverie. It's not just about complementing the gown, but harmonizing with the city's grandeur, the shimmering lights, and the dreams they've borne.

Join me, as we unravel the secrets whispered in the hallowed chambers of New York's elite salons, preparing those destined for the spotlight. For in Manhattan, a hairstyle isn't just an accessory; it's an assertion. As the flashbulbs pop and the world watches, remember: the Met staircase isn't just steps; it's a statement. Welcome to The Manhattan Diaries—where your tresses can tell tales as compelling as the city's most iconic tales.

The Met Gala: A Night of Manhattan Magic

In this city where dreams shine under the lights, we've unveiled the secrets of crafting hairstyles for the Met Gala. Each strand tells a story of elegance and drama, harmonizing with Manhattan's grandeur. As you savor the tales spun in New York's elite salons, remember that your tresses can tell compelling stories. The Met Gala isn't just an event; it's an experience where glamour, dreams, and hairstyling converge, leaving a mark on the city's narrative—a testament to the mystique of Manhattan. Welcome to The Manhattan Diaries, where every strand is a brushstroke on the canvas of the city's allure.

➢ **The Met Gala: A Night of Manhattan Magic**. In the heart of Manhattan, where the city's heartbeat synchronizes with the dreams of its denizens, we enter the spellbinding chapter of The Met Gala: A Night of Manhattan Magic. Here, amidst the shimmering lights and elegant soirees, uncover the enchantment and allure of one of the most prestigious events in the world—the Met Gala.

➢ **The Met Gala Extravaganza: A Manhattan Icon**. Dive into the grandeur of the Met Gala, an icon on Manhattan's social calendar. Explore how this star-studded event captivates the city's elite and the world with its opulence, fashion, and the promise of unforgettable moments.

➢ **The Red Carpet Spectacles: Where Dreams and Couture Collide**. Uncover the allure of the Met Gala's red carpet, where dreams and couture collide. Delve into the anticipation and excitement as celebrities and fashion icons ascend the steps, creating a mesmerizing spectacle that mirrors the city's magic.

> **The Art of Gala Styling: From Gowns to Tresses**. Understand the meticulous art of styling for the Met Gala, where gowns and tresses are carefully curated to harmonize with the year's theme. Explore how hairstylists play a pivotal role in creating the perfect ensemble, ensuring that every detail tells a story of elegance and sophistication.

> **The Met Gala: A Beacon of Style and Imagination**. Within the heart of Manhattan, the Met Gala stands as a beacon of style and imagination. It's a night where the city's elite, fashion luminaries, and celebrities converge, transcending the ordinary to celebrate the extraordinary. This illustrious gathering embodies the essence of Manhattan—an amalgamation of dreams, aspirations, and a relentless pursuit of beauty and elegance.

> **The Met Gala's Cultural Legacy: Shaping Manhattan's Narrative**. As the Met Gala unfolds year after year, its cultural legacy extends beyond fashion and art. The Met Gala is a reminder that Manhattan isn't just a place; it's a living, breathing entity.

> **Manhattan Dreams on Display: The Met Gala's Cultural Impact**. As we conclude our exploration, remember that the Met Gala isn't just an event; it's cultural phenomenon. Witness how it influences fashion trends, art, and conversations, leaving an indelible mark on Manhattan's narrative and the world's perception of the city.

In the dazzling realm of The Met Gala: A Night of Manhattan Magic, the city's allure reaches its zenith, and dreams materialize in the form of couture gowns, exquisite accessories, and meticulously coiffed tresses. The Met Gala isn't just an event; it's a celebration of Manhattan's essence—a city where style, imagination, and elegance converge, creating an enchanting narrative that transcends the ordinary and sets the stage for extraordinary moments.

Completed Tasks: Manhattan Magic Affair Activities

_____
_____
_____
_____
_____
_____
_____
_____
_____
_____
_____
_____
_____
_____
_____
_____
_____
_____
_____
_____
_____
_____
_____
_____
_____
_____
_____

Inspirational Quote

WE CAN'T HELP EVERYONE, BUT EVERYONE CAN HELP SOMEONE. —
Ronald Reagan

Action Items: Intentions and Thoughts

Hairstyling Alchemy: Crafting Red Carpet-Ready Tresses

In the heart of Manhattan's glamorous landscape, where the pursuit of perfection is an art form, we step into the captivating realm of Hairstyling Alchemy: Crafting Red Carpet-Ready Tresses. Here, amid the city's pulsating energy and shimmering lights, we'll unveil the secrets of transforming locks into masterpieces fit for the grandeur of the red carpet.

- ➢ **The Essence of Red Carpet Glamour: A Manhattan Tradition**. Embark on a journey into the essence of red carpet glamour, a tradition deeply ingrained in Manhattan's culture. Explore how this tradition isn't merely about walking the carpet; it's a profound art form that blends fashion, style, and the perfect coiffure into an unforgettable statement.

- ➢ **The Meticulous Art of Red Carpet Styling**. Enter the world of hairstylists who practice the meticulous art of red carpet styling. From old Hollywood waves that exude timeless elegance to avant-garde updos that challenge gravity itself, discover the skills and precision that transform tresses into iconic fashion accessories.

- ➢ **The Hair as a Signature: An Integral Element**. Understand that on the red carpet, hair isn't just an accessory—it's an integral element of the overall ensemble. Dive into the process of creating a harmonious symphony between gowns, accessories, and hairstyles, where each strand contributes to the wearer's unique signature of sophistication and allure.

- ➢ **Sculpting Manhattan's Tresses: The Artistry of Red Carpet Stylists**. Delve deeper into the world of hairstylists as they sculpt and shape Manhattan's tresses into mesmerizing forms. Explore their creative process, from envisioning the perfect look to meticulously bringing it to life, ensuring that every strand aligns with the wearer's personality and the event's grandeur.

➤ **The Collaborative Symphony: Hairstyling and Couture**. Uncover the harmonious collaboration between hairstylists and fashion designers in the realm of red carpet glamour. Discover how these creative minds work in tandem, ensuring that hairstyles and couture gowns not only complement each other but also create a visual symphony that leaves a lasting impression.

➤ **Tress Tale: Hairstyles That Whisper and Shout**. Explore the narrative power of red carpet hairstyles, where each coiffure has a voice. Whether it's a soft whisper of timeless elegance or a bold shout of avant-garde experimentation, these hairstyles convey messages of sophistication, confidence, and an unapologetic embrace of individuality.

➤ **Manhattan's Glamorous Legacy: Red Carpet Moments That Define an Era**. Reflect on the enduring legacy of Manhattan's red carpet moments, which have shaped fashion, beauty, and cultural conversations. From iconic looks that have become timeless classics to avant-garde creations that push the boundaries of style, these moments define eras and leave an indelible mark on the city's history.

➤ **Behind the Scenes: The Craft of Pre-Event Preparation**. Venture behind the scenes to discover the meticulous pre-event preparations that make red carpet hairstyles possible. From initial consultations to final touch-ups, this point sheds light on the crucial steps and backstage secrets that ensure every red carpet appearance is nothing short of spectacular.

As we conclude, remember that Hairstyling Alchemy: Crafting Red Carpet-Ready Tresses is more than artistry—it's the heart of Manhattan style. These hairstyles weave tales of elegance and drama, capturing the city's spirit and the dreams that shimmer beneath its skyline.

Completed Tasks: Red Carpet Hair Activities

_____

_____

_____

_____

_____

_____

_____

_____

_____

_____

_____

_____

_____

_____

_____

_____

_____

_____

_____

_____

_____

_____

_____

_____

_____

_____

_____

_____

_____

_____

Inspirational Quote

THE BEST WAY OUT IS ALWAYS THROUGH. — Robert Frost

Action Items: Intentions and Thoughts

Manhattan Metamorphosis: Hair as an Assertion

In the heart of Manhattan, where ambition and dreams intertwine like vines upon the city's skyscrapers, we step into the captivating chapter of Manhattan Metamorphosis: Hair as an Assertion. Here, amidst the urban symphony and the ever-pulsating energy, we'll explore the transformative power of hair, a silent yet assertive statement that defines the essence of Manhattan's elite.

- ➤ **Hair as a Manhattan Canvas: An Artistic Expression**. Delve into the idea that hair is more than just strands; it's a canvas for artistic expression. Discover how Manhattan's denizens use their hair to make a statement, from classic elegance to bold experimentation, reflecting their personalities and ambitions.

- ➤ **The Empowerment of Hairstyling: Confidence Beyond the Mirror**. Uncover the empowerment that hairstyling brings, where a carefully chosen hairstyle can instill confidence that transcends the reflection in the mirror. Explore how Manhattan's inhabitants use their coiffures to assert themselves in a city that demands nothing less than excellence.

- ➤ **From the Boardroom to the Gala: Hair's Role in Manhattan's Grand Narrative**. Understand how hair plays a pivotal role in shaping the grand narrative of Manhattan, whether it's a power bun in the boardroom or a cascading mane at a gala. Explore how these hairstyles become symbols of success, ambition, and the city's ever-evolving spirit.

- ➤ **Hair Icons of Manhattan: Inspirational Styles that Shape the City**. Explore the iconic hairstyles of Manhattan, from the polished bobs of Wall Street executives to the whimsical curls of artists in Greenwich Village. These hairstyles not only inspire but also define the neighborhoods and communities within the city, reflecting their unique identities and ambitions.

118

➤ **The Morning Ritual: Hairstyling as a Daily Affirmation**. Delve into the morning ritual of hairstyling for Manhattanites, where each brushstroke and curl is a daily affirmation of their confidence and readiness to conquer the urban jungle. Witness how this daily practice becomes a part of their identity and sets the tone for the day's challenges.

➤ **The Unspoken Language of Hair: Networking and Connections**. Understand the unspoken language of hair in Manhattan's networking circles. Hairstyles serve as conversation starters and icebreakers, forging connections and alliances in a city where relationships are often as valuable as currency.

➤ **The Future of Manhattan Hair: Trends and Aspirations**. Peek into the crystal ball to glimpse the future of Manhattan hair. Explore emerging trends and hairstyles that reflect the city's ever-evolving spirit and the aspirations of a new generation of Manhattanites, who continue to redefine what it means to assert oneself in the city that never sleeps.

➤ **The Manhattan Metamorphosis: A Personal and Collective Journey**. As we conclude our exploration, remember that Manhattan metamorphosis isn't just a personal journey; it's a collective one. Witness how the hairstyles of Manhattanites reflect not only their individual aspirations but also the city's ever-evolving identity, an assertion of their place within its captivating embrace.

With these statements, we immerse ourselves in the world of Manhattan Metamorphosis: Hair as an Assertion, where every hairstyle is a brushstroke on the canvas of self-expression and empowerment. Embrace the transformative power of hair as it weaves itself into the very fabric of Manhattan's allure, a testament to the city's relentless spirit and the dreams that flourish amidst its towering skyline.

Completed Tasks: Hair Metamorphosis Activities

Inspirational Quote

WITHOUT CRAFTSMANSHIP, INSPIRATION IS A MERE REED SHAKEN IN THE WIND. — Johannes Brahms

Action Items: Intentions and Thoughts

The Met Staircase: Where Tresses Tell Tales

In the heart of Manhattan, where dreams, aspirations, and artistry converge, we ascend the grand staircase of The Met—a place where history, culture, and style intertwine. But in this captivating chapter, we'll uncover a hidden facet of this iconic staircase—the tales whispered by the tresses that grace it. The Met Staircase: Where Tresses Tell Tales invites us into the world where hair isn't just an accessory but a storyteller, revealing the essence of Manhattan's elite.

➤ **The Met Staircase: A Stage of Elegance**. Enter the realm of The Met Staircase, where elegance is not just expected; it's the norm. Discover how the grandeur of this setting has inspired Manhattan's elite to elevate their hairstyling to an art form, where every step on the staircase is a graceful choreography of style and sophistication.

➤ **From Classic to Avant-Garde: Hairstyles of The Met**. Explore the diverse hairstyles that have graced The Met staircase over the years. From classic chignons that exude timeless elegance to avant-garde creations that challenge conventions, each coiffure is a statement—a piece of art that complements the wearer's personality and the theme of the event.

➤ **Tales Woven in Locks: The Personal Narratives**. Uncover the personal narratives woven into the locks of Manhattan's elite as they ascend The Met staircase. Each hairstyle tells a story—a tale of dreams, ambitions, and the desire to leave an indelible mark on the world. These narratives are whispered not in words but in the intricate twists and turns of their tresses.

➤ **Elegance Beyond the Exhibit: Tresses That Complement Art**. Explore how Manhattan's elite hairstylists carefully curate hairstyles that not only complement their attire but also resonate with the art on display at The Met. Witness the harmonious connection between artistic expression in fashion and hairstyling, where each stroke of the brush or curling iron becomes a work of art.

➢ **The Met's Themes: Hairstyles That Embody the Essence**. Dive into the intriguing world of how hairstyles are curated to embody the essence of The Met's annual themes. Whether it's channeling the elegance of the Victorian era or embracing the avant-garde spirit of Surrealism, these hairstyles become an integral part of the event's narrative, adding layers of depth and meaning to the experience.

➢ **Metropolitan Inspirations: Styles That Influence Manhattan's Elite**. Witness the symbiotic relationship between The Met's exhibitions and the hairstyles of Manhattan's elite. Discover how the art and culture showcased within the museum's walls inspire hairstylists and individuals alike, resulting in hairstyles that pay homage to the creativity and innovation found within The Met's collections.

➢ **The Met Staircase: A Confluence of Manhattan's Spirit**. As we conclude our exploration, remember that The Met staircase isn't just a physical location; it's a confluence of Manhattan's spirit, history, and aspirations. It's a reminder that in this city, every step is an opportunity to make a statement, and every hairstyle is a chapter in the ever-evolving story of its elite.

With these statements, we immerse ourselves in The Met Staircase: Where Tresses Tell Tales, where every strand is a brushstroke on the canvas of Manhattan's grand narrative. Witness how this iconic staircase transforms into a stage where hairstyles become the storytellers, weaving tales of elegance, individuality, and the enduring allure of the city that never sleeps.

Completed Tasks: Hair as Storyteller Activities

Inspirational Quote

LIFE IS NOT AN EXACT SCIENCE; IT IS AN ART. — Samuel Butler

Action Items: Intentions and Thoughts

Action Items: Intentions and Thoughts

SoHo Sleek:
Where Bohemian Meets Luxe

Manhattan, an urban tapestry where every street holds a narrative, where every corner whispers secrets of hopes, heartbreaks, and hallowed aspirations. And in this labyrinth of dreams, the journey is just as riveting as the destination—it's about the rhythm of your heels, the swing of your coat, and the sass that's quintessentially New York.

Picture it: You're sauntering down the cobbled lanes of SoHo, where cast-iron meets contemporary art. Eyes aren't just trailing the vintage Chanel you're donning but are ensnared by the captivating duality you exude. That, my dear, is the SoHo Sleek—a mesmerizing blend of bohemian free spirit and urbane luxury.

In this beguiling chapter of The Manhattan Diaries, we're diving deep into the mystique of SoHo, the enclave where artists' lofts coexist with high-end boutiques. From the casual elegance of a Parisian-inspired beret to the audaciousness of leather boots echoing through narrow streets, you'll learn to navigate the cityscape with both effortless boho chic and sharp metropolitan sophistication.

But remember, this isn't solely about fashion. It's a reflection of SoHo's soul—where gritty meets glamorous, where murals blend with marble. It's about becoming one with the city's dichotomy, where every brick has a tale, and every window reflects a dream.

Join me, as we journey through alleyways that have seen decades transform, felt paint strokes color their essence, and heard the murmurs of deals sealed over espressos. For in Manhattan, and especially in SoHo, your style doesn't just define you; it narrates a chapter of the city's ever-evolving story. So, take a breath, embrace the Sleek, and let SoHo serenade you. Welcome to The Manhattan Diaries—where every alley, every building, and every stride is a testament to a legacy of style.

The SoHo Aesthetic: Cobblestones and Canvas

In the heart of Manhattan, there exists a neighborhood that dances to the rhythm of artistic expression, where cobblestone streets meet the canvas of creativity. SoHo, short for South of Houston Street, is a district that embodies the very essence of New York City—where bohemian spirit collides with urban luxury, and where every step on its storied streets tells a tale or artistic vision and personal style.

> ➤ **Street Art Stories**. SoHo's walls are its storytellers, adorned with vibrant murals, graffiti masterpieces, and artistic expressions that change with the seasons. From internationally renowned artists to emerging talents, the neighborhood's facades are ever-evolving canvases that narrate the city's artistic pulse.

> ➤ **Boutiques and Bohemian Finds**. SoHo's boutiques are a treasure trove of fashion, where high-end luxury brands coexist with independent designers. Explore the cobblestone lanes to discover unique finds, from vintage gems to contemporary couture, all reflecting the neighborhood's eclectic taste.

> ➤ **Sidewalk Cafes and Urban Serenity**. SoHo's sidewalk cafes offer a slice of tranquility amidst the bustling city. Whether sipping espresso or people-watching, these cozy spots provide a respite where fashion merges with leisure, and style meets relaxation.

> ➤ **Artistic Evolution**. SoHo has witnessed the transformation of lofts into art studios, artists' sanctuaries where imagination knows no bounds. These spaces have birthed movements, challenged conventions, and contributed to the city's ever-evolving creative landscape.

> ➤ **The SoHo Experience**. Beyond the fashion and art, SoHo offers an experience that's uniquely New York. It's a place where historic

architecture stands alongside modern marvels, where the old world meets the avant-garde. The SoHo Aesthetic isn't just a look; it's a lifestyle, an attitude, and an artistic expression of self.

➤ **Leaving a Mark**. SoHo's influence extends beyond its borders. It has shaped the way we view urban aesthetics, fashion, and contemporary art. Its essence lingers in the hearts of those who have wandered its streets, leaving an indelible mark on their style and sensibilities.

➤ **Cobblestone Chronicles**. Explore SoHo's cobblestone streets, which not only add charm to the neighborhood but also serve as silent witnesses to its rich artistic heritage. Each stone paves the way through a district famed for its dynamic blend of art, fashion, and history.

➤ **Fashion Forward**. Delve into the heart of SoHo's fashion scene, where trendy boutiques and flagship stores set the trends. This neighborhood is a hotspot for fashion enthusiasts looking to capture a piece of Manhattan's chic, urban style.

To embrace The SoHo Aesthetic is to embrace the intersection of creativity and style, where every outfit is a form of self-expression and every street corner is a stage for artistry discovery. As you navigate the cobblestone streets and revel in the neighborhood's artistic charm, remember that in SoHo, your style becomes a canvas, and every step is a brushstroke in the grand narrative of this enchanting enclave.

In the SoHo Aesthetic, the city's soul comes alive, and the streets themselves become an ever-evolving work of art. Explore, express, and experience the magic that is SoHo—a place where cobblestones and canvas unite in a symphony of style and creativity.

Completed Tasks: Influencer Attitude Activities

_____

_____

_____

_____

_____

_____

_____

_____

_____

_____

_____

_____

_____

_____

_____

_____

_____

_____

_____

_____

_____

_____

_____

_____

_____

_____

_____

_____

Inspirational Quote

A HERO IS SOMEONE WHO HAS GIVEN HIS OR HER LIFE TO SOMETHING BIGGER THAN ONESELF. — Joseph Campbell

SOHO SLEEK

Action Items: Intentions and Thoughts

From Vintage Treasures to High-End Boutiques: SoHo's Retail Delights

In the bustling heart of Manhattan, where cobblestone streets intersect with contemporary flair, SoHo offers a shopping experience that's nothing short of extraordinary. From hidden vintage treasures that whisper tales of the past to high-end boutiques that showcase the latest in fashion, this neighborhood is a retail haven where style knows no boundaries.

> ➤ **Vintage Gems and Timeless Treasures**. SoHo's vintage boutiques are like time machines, offering curated collections of fashion from bygone eras. Unearth unique garments, accessories, and jewelry that tell stories of decades past, inviting you to make them a part of your own fashion narrative.

> ➤ **Designer Delights and Haute Couture**. For those seeking the pinnacle of fashion, SoHo's high-end boutiques beckon with a selection of designer labels and haute couture. Discover the latest runway trends and timeless classics, ensuring that your wardrobe reflects the essence of Manhattan's style.

> ➤ **Artisanal Craftsmanship and Unique Finds**. SoHo is a haven for those who appreciate the artistry of fashion. Explore independent boutiques that showcase artisanal craftsmanship, whether it's hand-stitched leather goods, bespoke jewelry, or one-of-a-kind accessories. Here, individuality is celebrated, and each piece is a work of art.

> ➤ **Home and Lifestyle Boutiques**. Beyond fashion, SoHo boasts a vibrant collection of home and lifestyle boutiques. Embark on a journey through stores offering unique furnishings, decor, and lifestyle essentials, allowing you to infuse your living spaces with the same artistic spirit that defines the neighborhood.

➤ **A Shopping Experience Like No Other**. SoHo's retail scene isn't just about shopping; it's an immersive experience. As you navigate its streets, you'll encounter historic buildings transformed into stylish storefronts, and each boutique has its own distinct personality, offering a glimpse into the neighborhood's eclectic taste.

➤ **Elevating Your Style**. SoHo's retail delights go beyond clothing; they elevate your style and infuse it with the essence of the city. From vintage discoveries that add a touch of nostalgia to contemporary couture that sets the trend, SoHo has the power to transform your wardrobe and leave an indelible mark on your fashion sense.

➤ **Embrace the SoHo Shopping Vibe**. To embrace SoHo's retrial delights is to embrace the convergence of fashion, art, and individuality. As you explore the boutiques and uncover unique pieces that resonate with your style, you become part of a narrative that celebrates the beauty of self-expression and the allure of SoHo's retail charm.

➤ **Cultural Corners**. Delve into the diverse cultural corners of SoHo, where each boutique not only sells fashion but also represents the myriad cultures that the neighborhood embraces. These shops offer more than just merchandise; they provide a window into the global influences that shape SoHo's unique style.

➤ **Seasonal Style Festivals**. Participate in SoHo's seasonal style festivals, where the streets come alive with fashion shows, pop-up shops, and exclusive releases.

In SoHo, shopping isn't just a transaction; it's an expression of personal style and a celebration of the neighborhood's artistic spirit. It's an invitation to explore, discover, and adorn yourself with the stories and creations that make SoHo a retail paradise like no other.

Completed Tasks: Retail Havens Activities

Inspirational Quote

WHAT WE ACHIEVE INWARDLY WILL CHANGE OUTER REALITY. — Plutarch

Action Items: Intentions and Thoughts

Street Art as Fashion Inspiration: Murals and Muses

In the eclectic heart of Manhattan's SoHo district, where cobblestone streets and creativity collide, there's a captivating synergy between art and fashion. The neighborhood's vibrant street art scene is more than just murals adorning walls; it's a wellspring of inspiration for style mavens who understand that fashion and art are inseparable.

➢ **A Canvas of Colorful Expression**. SoHo's streets serve as a canvas for artists from around the world. The neighborhood's walls breathe with life, adorned by murals that range from abstract bursts of color to intricate portraits. Each stroke of paint becomes a source of inspiration for fashionistas seeking to infuse their style with artistic flair.

➢ **Street Art Chic: Bold Statements**. SoHo's street art often finds its way into fashion statements. From graffiti-inspired prints on clothing to accessories that pay homage to iconic murals, incorporating street art into your ensemble is a bold way to showcase your appreciation for the neighborhood's creative spirit.

➢ **Sunglasses and Street Style**. SoHo's streets aren't just a place to admire art; they're a runway for street style. Fashion-forward individuals don their most daring outfits, often accessorized with statement sunglasses, as they stroll amidst the murals. Here, style becomes a form of self-expression, and every passerby is a muse.

➢ **Artful Accessories and Urban Edge**. SoHo's boutiques feature accessories that reflect the neighborhood's artistic vibe. Discover handbags and jewelry that incorporate elements of street art, adding an urban edge to your ensemble. These pieces are not just accessories; they're wearable art.

➢ **Inspiration on Every Corner.** In SoHo, every street corner holds artistic surprises. Whether it's a thought-provoking quote stenciled on a sidewalk or a mural that captures the essence of the neighborhood, you'll find inspiration everywhere you look. It's a reminder that fashion is a reflection of the world around us.

➢ **Walking Art Gallery.** SoHo's streets transform into a walking art gallery, where the murals serve as a backdrop for fashion shoots and street photography. The neighborhood's ever-changing art scene provides an ever-evolving visual narrative for those who appreciate the synergy of art and style.

➢ **Becoming Part of the Narrative.** To embrace street art as fashion inspiration in SoHo is to become part of the neighborhood's creative narrative. It's a way of infusing your style with the energy and individuality that define the district, making your fashion choices an artistic expression of self.

➢ **Designer Collaborations with Street Artists.** Explore the exciting collaborations between SoHo's street artists and fashion designers. These partnerships produce unique collections that blend high fashion with the raw, visceral energy of street art, offering pieces that are as much about wearable art as they are about high-end style.

➢ **Interactive Fashion Installations.** Participate in interactive fashion installations inspired by SoHo's street art. These events combine live mural painting with dynamic fashion displays, allowing attendees to engage directly with the creative process and witness the fusion of contemporary art and fashion in real-time.

In SoHo, the streets themselves are an ever-changing work of art, and every outfit and hairstyle becomes a canvas for personal expression. As you wander through this artistic enclave, let the murals be your muses, and fashion your medium of creative storytelling.

Completed Tasks: Fashion and Art Activities

Inspirational Quote

LET US DREAM OF TOMORROW WHERE WE CAN TRULY LOVE FROM THE SOUL AND KNOW LOVE AS THE ULTIMATE TRUTH AT THE HEART OF ALL CREATION. — Michael Jackson

Action Items: Intentions and Thoughts

The SoHo State of Mind: Embracing Dichotomy with Flair

In the heart of Manhattan's SoHo district, where historic cobblestone streets meet contemporary creativity, there exists a unique state of mind. It's a mindset that thrives on embracing the delightful contradictions of urban living, a dichotomy that infuses every aspect of life with unmistakable flair.

➢ **Historic Charm and Modern Elegance**. SoHo is a place where 19th century cast-iron facades harmoniously coexist with cutting-edge modernity. Its streets are a living testament to the seamless blend of history and innovation, and this duality is reflected in the fashion choices of those who call it home.

➢ **Artistic Reverie and Urban Reality**. SoHo's streets are adorned with vibrant murals and street art, creating a whimsical dreamscape. Yet, beneath this artistic reverie lies the urban reality of city life. Fashion in SoHo often strikes a balance between embracing the imaginative and navigating the everyday.

➢ **Bohemian Freedom and Metropolitan Chic**. SoHo is a place where bohemian free spirits and metropolitan chic coexist harmoniously. The fashion scene here effortlessly marries the unconventional with the sophisticated, resulting in ensembles that defy categorization.

➢ **Natural Beauty and Urban Glamour**. SoHo's style is a reflection of its surroundings. Just as the neighborhood's parks and green spaces provide a respite from the city's hustle, fashion choices here can seamlessly transition from natural beauty to urban glamour, mirroring the dichotomy of the urban oasis.

➢ **Nightlife Revelry and Quiet Retreats**. SoHo's nightlife is vibrant and electrifying, with stylish denizens embracing the allure of the city after dark. Yet, within this lively scene, there's an appreciation for quiet retreats—intimate cafes, art galleries, and hidden corners where conversations flow as effortlessly as fashion choices.

> **Elevated Basics and Avant-Garde Pieces**. SoHo's fashion philosophy encompasses both elevated basics that exude timeless elegance and avant-garde pieces that push the boundaries of style. The result is a wardrobe that effortlessly transitions from casual to couture.

> **An Elegantly Dichotomous Lifestyle**. Living in SoHo is an elegantly dichotomous experience. It's about savoring leisurely brunches at charming cafes while also navigating the fast-paced urban landscape. Fashion in SoHo is an extensions of this lifestyle, embracing the juxtapositions that define the neighborhood.

> **Cultural Fusion and Cosmopolitan Exclusivity**. SoHo is a melting pot of cultures, where global influences merge to create a cosmopolitan tapestry reflected in its fashion scene. Explore how SoHo's diverse cultural elements are woven into the fabric of its everyday style, from ethnic prints to haute couture, celebrating a worldliness that is uniquely New York.

> **Seamless Indoor-Outdoor Living**. Reflecting SoHo's architectural openness with its abundant lofts and large windows, fashion too plays with concepts of indoor and outdoor living. Garments are versatile, blending comfort with chic, suitable for gallery hopping or rooftop gatherings, embodying the neighborhood's fluid lifestyle dynamics.

In SoHo, embracing the state of mind means understanding that life's richness lies in its contradictions. Fashion becomes a canvas where individuals can paint their unique stories, unburdened by the need for conformity. It's about celebrating the duality of city life with flair, where every outfit tells a tale of SoHo's enchanting dichotomy.

Completed Tasks: City Life with Flair Activities

Inspirational Quote

THE QUALITY, NOT THE LONGEVITY OF ONE'S LIFE IS WHAT IS IMPORTANT.
— Martin Luther King Jr.

142

Action Items: Intentions and Thoughts

Legacy of Style: SoHo's Ever-Evolving Story

Nestled in the heart of Manhattan, SoHo is not just a neighborhood—it's a living testament to the ever-evolving narrative of style. Its cobblestone streets have borne witness to the fashion metamorphosis of a city that never sleeps, where the legacy of style continues to unfold.

> ➢ **The Birth of Urban Chic**. SoHo emerged from the ashes of its industrial past to become a hotbed of urban chic. The neighborhood's converted loft spaces became the canvas for artistic expression, setting the stage for a style renaissance that celebrated individuality and creativity.

> ➢ **From Artistic Enclave to Fashion Hub**. SoHo's transformation from an artistic enclave to a fashion hub was a natural progression. As galleries and studios gave way to boutiques and flagship stores, the neighborhood's style evolved from bohemian to high-end, embracing a spectrum of tastes and trends.

> ➢ **Iconic Boutiques and Flagship Stores**. SoHo's streets are lined with iconic boutiques and flagship stores of renowned fashion brands. It's a shopping destination that marries heritage and innovation, offering a curated selection of fashion pieces that tell stories of both tradition and trendsetting.

> ➢ **Street Style as an Art Form**. Street style in SoHo is not just a reflection of fashion—it's an art form in itself. The neighborhood's denizens effortlessly blend vintage finds with contemporary couture, creating ensembles that blur the lines between everyday life and high fashion.

> ➢ **The Influence of Social Media**. The rise of social media has catapulted SoHo's fashion legacy onto a global state. Instagram-worthy moments abound, from street art backdrops to stylish

brunch spots, making SoHo a magnet for influencers and trendsetters.

➢ **Sustainability and Ethical Fashion**. SoHo's commitment to style extends beyond aesthetics. The neighborhood has embraced sustainability and ethical fashion, with boutiques showcasing eco-friendly designs and responsible sourcing, reflecting a shift toward conscious consumption.

➢ **Beauty and Beyond**. SoHo isn't just about fashion; it's a beauty destination too. The neighborhood's salons and spas cater to those who seek not just style but also self-care offering a holistic approach to personal grooming.

➢ **A Legacy Continues**. The legacy of style in SoHo continues to evolve, adapting to the changing needs and desires of its diverse denizens. As new generations of trendsetters call this neighborhood home, they add their chapters to its fashion story, ensuring that the legacy remains as vibrant as ever.

➢ **Cultural Revivals and Collaborative Spaces**. SoHo's legacy of style is continually rejuvenated through cultural revivals and the creation of collaborative spaces that foster innovation across fashion, art, and technology. These venues serve as incubators for new ideas, where established designers and emerging talents converge to experiment and redefine the boundaries of style, pushing SoHo to the forefront of global fashion trends.

In SoHo, style isn't confined to runways or red carpets—it's an intrinsic part of everyday life. As the neighborhood's legacy of style evolves, it serves as a reminder that fashion is not just about clothing; it's a form of self-expression and a reflection of the times. SoHo's ever-evolving story of style is a testament to the enduring allure of fashion in the heart of New York City.

Completed Tasks: Legacy of Style Activities

Action Items: Intentions and Thoughts

Action Items: Intentions and Thoughts

Midnight Manes:
Taming Your Hair for After-Hour Soirees

Manhattan, an electrifying mosaic of shimmering city lights and dreams that refuse to dim, even as the clock strikes twelve o'clock. Here, every twilight is a prologue to a story—of rendezvous, of whispered confidences, of champagne toasts. In the city that never sleeps, it's not just about arriving—it's about making an entrance, with flair, finesse, and that fabulous hair.

Envision this: You're descending the steps of a hidden speakeasy, the pulse of jazz palpable in the air. All eyes shift, not merely due to the elegance of your ensemble, but the cascading waves of your hair, reflecting the city lights. That, darling, is the Midnight Mane—a crowning glory that speaks of mystery, allure, and a touch of nocturnal magic.

In this tantalizing chapter of The Manhattan Diaries, we'll delve into the art of crafting that perfect after-hour hairstyle. From the sultry loose curls that dance with every step to the sleek bun that means serious business, every twist, every turn, every pin has a secret to tell.

Yet, it's more than just a hairstyle—it's a statement. It's about embracing the vibrancy of Manhattan nights, where every heartbeat syncs with the rhythm of street musicians, and the city's skyline becomes a constellation of its own.

Journey with me, as we navigate through the dimly lit bars, the rooftop lounges, the moonlit piers, all the while ensuring your mane is not just a style but an experience. Because in Manhattan, when the sun sets, a new world awakens—one where your tresses tell tales as intriguing as the city's nocturnal secrets. Welcome to The Manhattan Diaries, where, come midnight, your mane becomes a tale as timeless as the city's skyline.

The Nighttime Alchemy of Hair

In the glittering heart of Manhattan, as the sun bids adieu to the day and the city's skyline transforms into a constellation of dreams, a magical alchemy unfolds. It's a transformation that gives birth to a different Manhattan, one where the streets become pathways to enchantment, and every rooftop bar holds the promise of secrets yet to be revealed. Amidst this electric ambiance, there exists a silent protagonist—the hair, your hair. It becomes a canvas upon which the night's enchantment is painted, a testament to the city's alluring after-hours charm.

> ➤ **The Midnight Mane: Cascading Waves of Enchantment**. As you descend the steps of a clandestine speakeasy, the haunting melodies of jazz serenade your senses. Heads turn, not merely in admiration of your chic ensemble but in awe of the cascading waves of your hair, illuminated by the city's twinkling lights. That, darling, is the Midnight Mane—a crown of glory that speaks volumes of mystique, allure, and a dash of midnight magic.

> ➤ **Manhattan's Nocturnal Transformation: A City Reborn After Dark**. In this intoxicating chapter of Manhattan's nightlife, we embark on a journey through the city's nocturnal pulse, where every street corner holds the promise of enchantment, and every rooftop bar whispers its secrets. It's a realm where your hair isn't just a style but a vital player in the unfolding drama of the night. It's the finishing touch that sets the stage for a night of Manhattan's nocturnal enchantment.

> ➤ **The Artistry of Midnight Hairstyling: Wielding Brushes as Wands**. As the city undergoes its nightly metamorphosis, hairstylists in Manhattan's upscale salons become modern-day alchemists. With their brushes and combs, they wield the power to transform your daytime appearance into a nighttime masterpiece. Loose curls that

150

dance with each step infuse sensuality into your persona, while the sleek bun exudes sophistication and power. It's not just about a hairstyle; it's about readiness for whatever the night may bring.

➢ **Nocturnal Whispers: Your Hair, the Silent Witness**. In Manhattan, where the city's heartbeat syncs with the rhythm of street musicians and the skyline becomes a celestial tapestry, your hair becomes more than just an accessory. It becomes a confidant, a silent witness to secrets shared and dreams woven into the fabric of the night. Your Midnight Mane narrates tales as intriguing as the city's most closely guarded nocturnal secrets.

➢ **The Seductive Whispers of the Night: From Sunset to Twilight, Your Hair's Journey**. As the sun sets over the city, your hair begins its transformation, evolving from the daytime's elegance to the nighttime's seductive allure. Whether it's tousled waves or a sleek updo, your Midnight Mane is a reflection of your journey through Manhattan's twilight hours.

➢ **Hairstyling Elixir: The Craftsmanship Behind the Magic**. Behind the scenes, hairstylists in Manhattan's elite salons work their magic, crafting the perfect nighttime hairstyles that complement your ensemble and match the city's electrifying ambiance. It's a fusion of skill, creativity, and a touch of Manhattan's enchantment.

Welcome to the section dedicated to the Nighttime Alchemy of Hair, where the night belongs to the stars, the secrets, and the allure of your Midnight Mane. In this chapter, we celebrate the art of nighttime alchemy, where your hair takes center stage in the mesmerizing drama of Manhattan's nocturnal glamour. It's a world where every strand of hair weaves a story as captivating as the city's nocturnal secrets.

Completed Tasks: Nighttime Hair Activities

Inspirational Quote

BE NOT ENTANGLED IN THIS WORLD OF DAYS AND NIGHTS; THOU HAST
ANOTHER TIME AND SPACE AS WELL. — Muhammad Iqbal

Action Items: Intentions and Thoughts

Hair as an Entrance Ticket

In the heart of Manhattan, the night holds an intoxicating allure. The city's skyline comes alive with a tapestry of lights, and the streets pulsate with energy. It's a realm where dreams are realized, secrets are shared, and the line between reality and fantasy blurs. In this nocturnal wonderland, your hair becomes more than just a style—it's your entrance ticket to the most exclusive soirees and clandestine speakeasies. As we delve into the enchanting world of Manhattan's nightlife, let's explore how your Midnight Mane is your ultimate accessory, your statement of intent, and your key to unlocking the city's hidden treasures.

- ➤ **The Night's Canvas: Crafting the Perfect Midnight Mane**. When the sun dips below the horizon, Manhattan's finest salons come alive with the artistry of hairstylists who understand the essence of nighttime glamour. From tousled curls that dance with the city's rhythm to sleek updos that exude sophistication, your Midnight Mane is meticulously crafted to complement your ensemble and accentuate your allure. It's the result of a collaboration between you and your stylist, a masterpiece that sets the stage for your night of enchantment.

- ➤ **Twilight Whispers: Secrets Shared in the Dim Light**. As you step into Manhattan's nightlife, your Midnight Mane becomes a silent confidante, privy to the secrets whispered in dimly lit bars and hidden corners. It frames your face as you engage in intimate conversations, it shimmers under the glow of candlelight during romantic dinners, and it catches the eye of fellow night owls who appreciate the art of seduction. Your hair tells a story of intrigue, of encounters that leave an indelible mark on your memory.

- ➤ **The Elegance of the Night: Manhattan's Nocturnal Playground**. Manhattan's nightlife is a playground for the elegant, the daring, and the adventurous. Your Midnight Mane is your emblem, your signal to the world that you're ready to embrace the city's nocturnal charms. It's a reflection of your confidence, your style, and your readiness to dance until dawn. As you move through the city's twilight, remember that your hair is more than just strands—it's an expression of your Manhattan spirit.

➢ **A Night to Remember: Making Memories under the Stars**. In the city that never sleeps, every night holds the promise of unforgettable memories. Your Midnight Mane is there to witness it all, from the laughter shared with friends to the chance encounters that ignite sparks of romance. As the night unfolds, your hair captures the essence of each moment, ensuring that the memories you create are as timeless as the city itself.

➢ **The Art of Transformation**. Your Midnight Mane isn't just a hairstyle; it's a transformation. It can take you from a daytime professional to a nighttime enchantress with a few expertly placed pins and curls. It's a testament to the versatility of Manhattan's nightlife, where reinvention is an art form.

➢ **A Whirlwind of Styles**. Manhattan's nightlife isn't monotonous, and neither should your Midnight Mane be. Explore a spectrum of styles, from classic Hollywood waves to edgy punk-inspired updos. Each style represents a facet of your personality.

As the clock ticks and the city's heartbeat grows stronger, your Midnight Mane takes center stage in Manhattan's nightlife. It's a symbol of your presence, your participation in the city's vibrant nocturnal tapestry. So, embrace the allure of the night, let your hair speak volumes, and dance to the rhythm of Manhattan's starlit streets. Welcome to the world where your Midnight Mane is your ultimate entrance ticket—a key to unlocking the enchantment of the city that never sleeps.

Completed Tasks: Entrance Ticket Hair Activities

Inspirational Quote

THERE IS ONLY ONE DIFFERENCE BETWEEN A LONG LIFE AND A GOOD DINNER: THAT, IN THE DINNER, THE SWEETS COME LAST. — Robert Louis Stevenson

MIDNIGHT MANES

Action Items: Intentions and Thoughts

Nocturnal Magic in Every Strand

In the city that never sleeps, every night holds the promise of enchantment and intrigue. Manhattan's nocturnal world is a canvas of sparkling city lights, hidden speakeasies, and whispered secrets that come alive after the sun sets. And at the heart of this captivating nightlife is the art of hairstyling, where every strand of hair becomes a brushstroke in the masterpiece of the night. Welcome to the world of Nocturnal Magic in Every Strand, where we explore the transformative power of nighttime hairstyles.

➤ **The Midnight Mane**. Your hair becomes a canvas for creativity as you craft the perfect Midnight Mane. Whether it's sultry waves, a sleek updo, or a daring braid, your choice of hairstyle sets the tone for the night ahead. It's not just about looking fabulous; it's about embracing the mystique of Manhattan's nightlife.

➤ **Dancing Under the Stars**. Manhattan's nighttime adventures can take you from rooftop parties with panoramic city views to intimate jazz clubs where the music sways your soul. With the right hairstyle, you'll feel like you're dancing under the stars, your hair catching the moonlight and the city's effervescent energy.

➤ **Secrets of the Night**. As the night unfolds, your Midnight Mane becomes a keeper of secrets. It whispers stories of chance encounters, stolen glances, and unforgettable moments. It's a testament to the allure of the city, where anything can happen, and your hair is there to witness it all.

➤ **Confidence in the Dark**. There's a unique confidence that comes with knowing your hair is on point, even in the darkest corners of Manhattan. Whether you're mingling with artists in hidden galleries or strolling through cobblestone streets, your Midnight Mane is your ticket to feeling like you belong in this nocturnal wonderland.

➢ **The Essence of Seduction**. Your Midnight Mane is more than just a hairstyle; it's a seductive allure that draws people into your orbit. Whether you're sipping cocktails at a swanky lounge or engaging in witty banter at a clandestine bar, your hair becomes a conversation starter, a magnetic force that leaves a lasting impression.

➢ **Romance in Every Strand**. Manhattan nights are imbued with romance, and your hair becomes a symbol of that romance. It's the soft curls that frame your face as you share a candlelit dinner or the tousled waves that catch the breeze during a moonlit stroll in Central Park. Your hair becomes a poetic element in the love stories written in the city's heart.

➢ **The Confidence Boost**. There's a certain confidence that comes from knowing your hair is impeccable. It's like having a secret weapon in the world of Manhattan's nightlife. Whether you're navigating a crowded dance floor or making a grand entrance at a glamorous gala, your Midnight Mane gives you the self-assuredness to conquer the night.

➢ **A Chapter in the Night's Tale**. Your hairstyle becomes a chapter in the story of the night. It evolves with each adventure, from the tousled locks of a midnight motorcycle ride to the elegant updo of a soiree at a penthouse terrace. Your Midnight Mane adapts to the twists and turns of the night, reflecting the ever-changing narrative of Manhattan's nocturnal world.

In Nocturnal Magic in Every Strand, we've uncover the artistry behind creating the perfect nighttime hairstyle and the role it plays in shaping your Manhattan nights. So, let your hair down, embrace the allure of the night, and let your Midnight Mane weave its own spell in the city that never sleeps.

Completed Tasks: Nocturnal Magic Activities

Inspirational Quote

I PRAY GOD MAY PRESERVE YOUR HEALTH AND LIFE MANY YEARS. —
Junipero Serra

Action Items: Intentions and Thoughts

Tales as Timeless as the City's Skyline

Manhattan, a city of endless stories, where each glimmering skyscraper and bustling street corner holds secrets and tales waiting to be told. In this metropolis, where dreams and reality intertwine, your Midnight Mane becomes more than just hair—it's a reflection of the stories you create, the memories you cherish, and the nights that define your Manhattan journey.

> ➤ **Unveiling the Stories: The Rooftop Romance**. Your midnight Mane is the backdrop to those rooftop rendezvous, where the city lights twinkle like stars above, and the skyline becomes a canvas for your love story. It's the tousled waves that catch the moonlight as you steal a kiss against the backdrop of the Empire State Building.

> ➤ **The Speakeasy Whispers**. In dimly lit speakeasies hidden behind unassuming facades, your hair becomes a silent confidante to the secrets exchanged over vintage cocktails. It's the sleek bun that conceals the intrigue in your eyes as you navigate a clandestine world of whispered conversations and forbidden allure.

> ➤ **The Midnight Strolls**. As you wander the city's streets in the witching hour, your Midnight Mane flows with a certain mystique. It's the embodiment of Manhattan's nocturnal energy, the tangle of loose curls that dances with the night breeze, and the tousled locks that capture the essence of urban exploration.

> ➤ **The Gala Glamour**. At exclusive galas and black-tie affairs, your hair becomes a work of art, a masterpiece that rivals the grandeur of the city's iconic landmarks. It's the intricate updo adorned with diamonds and pearls that commands attention as you ascend the grand staircase of a Manhattan institution.

> ➤ **A Testament to Timelessness**. In a city where time moves at its own pace, your Midnight Mane serves as a testament to the timeless

allure of Manhattan nights. It's a reminder that while the city evolves and changes, certain elements remain constant—the magic of the night, the allure of the skyline, and the stories written in the strands of your hair. Each Midnight Mane is a chapter in the ongoing narrative of Manhattan, tales that endure as long as the city's skyline stands tall.

➤ **The Moonlit Serenade**. Your Midnight Mane takes center stage during moonlit serenades in Central Park, where the notes of a saxophone mingle with the rustling leaves. It's the graceful updo that harmonizes with the melodies, making you a part of the city's nocturnal symphony.

➤ **The Art Gallery Soirees**. At exclusive art gallery soirees, your hair becomes a work of art itself, a canvas that reflects the creativity and innovation of the city's artistic elite. It's the braided masterpiece that draws admiration from fellow patrons and becomes a conversation starter about the intersection of fashion and art.

➤ **The Late-Night Revelry**. In the heart of Manhattan's nightlife, your Midnight Mane stands out as a beacon of style and sophistication. It's the sleek and glossy ponytail that keeps up with your dance moves at trendy clubs, reflecting the city's pulsating energy and endless possibilities.

So, as you venture into the midnight realm of Manhattan, remember that your Midnight Mane is not just a hairstyle; it's a living, breathing part of the city's story. It captures the essence of the night, the allure of the city, and the tales as timeless as the Manhattan skyline itself. Welcome to The Manhattan Diaries, where your Midnight Mane becomes a legend in the city's ever-evolving tale.

Completed Tasks: Midnight Stories Activities

_____
_____
_____
_____
_____
_____
_____
_____
_____
_____
_____
_____
_____
_____
_____
_____
_____
_____
_____
_____
_____
_____
_____
_____
_____
_____

Inspirational Quote

GOD ALWAYS GIVES HIS BEST TO THOSE WHO LEAVE THE CHOICE WITH HIM. — Jim Elliot

Action Items: Intentions and Thoughts

Action Items: Intentions and Thoughts

Brooklyn to Broadway: A Journey of Diverse Hair Inspirations

Manhattan, a radiant beacon of dreams, where bridges not only connect boroughs but weave stories that span across generations, cultures, and styles. Amidst the hum of cabs and the lullaby of Broadway, it's not merely about setting the scene—it's about stealing the show, from head to toe, and especially from root to tip.

Visualize this: You're stepping off the subway, ascending from the depths of Brooklyn's gritty charm, and emerging into the glittering heart of Times Square. And while the neon lights might be dazzling, it's your hair that becomes the talk of the town. That, my dear, is the Brooklyn to Broadway transition—an evolution of style that blends urban edge with theatrical flair.

In this captivating chapter of the Manhattan Diaries, we trace the journey of tresses inspired by the brownstones of Brooklyn to the marquees of Broadway. Whether it's the braids echoing tales from Bed-Stuy or the dramatic updos worthy of a standing ovation, each strand tells a story of diversity, defiance, and drama.

But remember, it's never just about a hairstyle—it's an odyssey. A journey that celebrates the mosaic that is Manhattan, where every neighborhood has its narrative, every corner its character. It's about embracing the juxtaposition of street art and stage lights, understanding the symphony of the city.

Accompany me, as we traverse the boroughs, letting each wind, each whisper, each note, shape our style. Because in Manhattan, and its extended family, every day is an opportunity for transformation, a metamorphosis awaiting its moment. Welcome to The Manhattan Diaries, where your hair narrates tales as vast and varied as the city's skyline.

Borough-Inspired Styles

In the city that never sleeps, every neighborhood in Manhattan has its own unique character, flair, and sense of style. From the gritty charm of Brooklyn to the dazzling lights of Broadway, the diversity of influences is reflected in the hairstyles that grace the bustling streets. Join me as we explore the borough-inspired styles that make Manhattan's hair scene a captivating tale of transformation and self-expression.

➤ **Bed-Stuy Braids: A Tribute to Brooklyn Roots**. Bed-Stuy, the heart of Brooklyn, inspires hairstyles that pay homage to its rich cultural heritage. Braids become a symbol of strength, unity, and storytelling within the community. Each braid tells a story of resilience and diversity, reflecting the neighborhood's vibrant spirit.

➤ **Harlem Elegance: A Renaissance-Inspired Revival**. Harlem's rich history and artistic heritage inspired hairstyles are reminiscent of the Harlem Renaissance. Elegance and sophistication are the hallmarks of these hairstyles, reflecting a sense of pride and cultural heritage. Each twist and turn of the hair embodies the legacy of this iconic neighborhood.

➤ **Theatrical Glamour: Broadway's Dramatic Updos**. As we venture closer to Broadway, the hairstyles take on a dramatic flair fit for the stage. Updos steal the show, reflecting the theatrical magic that defines this district. Every strand is a performer, ready to take center stage and command attention.

➤ **Manhattan's Mosaic of Styles: Embracing Diversity**. Manhattan's neighborhoods form a unique mosaic of cultures, and the hairstyles mirror this diversity. The city's streets are a runway for self-expression, where individuality shines. From Brooklyn to Broadway, hair becomes a canvas for storytelling, bridging gaps and celebrating the rich tapestry of Manhattan.

168

➤ **East Village Edge: Embracing Bohemian Chic**. The East Village, a hotbed of artistic creativity and individualism, inspires hairstyles that embody bohemian chic. Loose waves, tousled curls, and effortless braids capture the free-spirited essence of this neighborhood. These hairstyles are a nod to the avant-garde and unconventional, making a statement that sets you apart in the heart of the East Village.

➤ **Financial District Finesse: Sleek and Polished Power Styles**. In the Financial District, where ambition and success reign supreme, sleek and polished power styles take center stage. These hairstyles exude confidence and authority, aligning perfectly with the corporate world that thrives in this bustling neighborhood. Each strand is meticulously styled to reflect ambition, making these hairstyles a symbol of determination and ambition.

➤ **Chinatown Charm: Cultural Fusion in Hair Art**. The vibrant cultural fusion of Chinatown inspires hairstyles that celebrate diversity and tradition. Elaborate hair ornaments, intricate bun styles, and symbolic hair accessories pay homage to the neighborhood's rich heritage.

➤ **Greenwich Village Vibes: Retro Revival and Boho Beauty**. Greenwich Village, known for its counterculture movements, inspires hairstyles that blend retro revival with boho beauty.

In this city of endless possibilities, your hair becomes a testament to the dynamic spirit of Manhattan. Each style weaves a narrative of resilience, heritage, and drama, mirroring the neighborhoods that inspire them. As we embark on this journey, remember that in Manhattan, every day is an opportunity for transformation, and your hair is the ultimate expression of that metamorphosis. Welcome to a world where your tresses tell tales as diverse and captivating as the city's skyline itself.

Completed Tasks: Borough-Inspired Styles Activities

Inspirational Quote

HEALTH IS THE GREATEST GIFT, CONTENTMENT THE GREATEST WEALTH, FAITHFULNESS THE BEST RELATIONSHIP — Buddha

Action Items: Intentions and Thoughts

The Broadway Glamour

Broadway, the enchanting heart of Manhattan's theatrical dreams, where the spotlight shines as bright as the city's hopes. In this illustrious district where stories unfold on the grandest stages, it's not just about the performance— it's about the allure, the elegance, and, of course, the glamour.

> ➤ **Theatre-Inspired Tresses**. Transport yourself to the golden age of theater with the vintage Hollywood waves, iconic waves that exude timeless elegance. Or push the boundaries of style with dramatic updos that capture the essence of Broadway's creativity.

> ➤ **Hairstyling as Character**. Discover how hairstyling becomes an integral part of embodying a character on the stage. Explore how hairstyles contribute to the narrative and emotional depth of a theatrical performance.

> ➤ **Backstage Beauty**. Peek behind the curtains into the dressing rooms and backstage sanctuaries where hairstylists work their magic. Learn how professionals craft the perfect hairstyle to complement thespians and stars under the bright lights of Broadway.

> ➤ **Behind-the-Scenes Drama**. The world of hairstylists behind Broadway's curtains is a realm of high-stakes preparation, where every strand must align with precision. These unsung heroes work tirelessly to ensure that performers shine on stage. Their backstage challenges include navigating quick changes, managing intricate hairpieces, and coping with the ever-present pressure of perfection. It's a captivating world where creativity meets chaos, and where the magic of hair transformation happens behind closed doors.

> ➤ **Iconic Broadway Hair**. As we venture further into the heart of Broadway, we uncover the iconic hairstyles that have left an indelible mark on both the stage and popular culture. From the glamorous

finger waves of the '20s to the punk-inspired looks of the '90s and beyond, each era in Broadway's history has brought forth hairstyles that tell stories about the characters, settings, and times they represent. These hairstyles are not just adornments but essential elements that transport audiences to different worlds.

➢ **The Evolution of Broadway Hairstyles**. Broadway is a living archive of hairstyling trends, reflecting the changing aesthetics and societal norms of different eras. From the classic elegance of the mid-20th century to the more experimental and inclusive styles of contemporary productions, the evolution of Broadway hairstyles mirrors the evolution of society. It's a fascinating journey through time, where hair becomes a visual chronicle of our cultural history.

➢ **Costume and Coiffure**. In the world of Broadway, costumes and hairstyles are inextricably linked. They work in tandem to create the overall look and feel of a production, transporting audiences to different times and places. It's a synergy where every detail matters, and the harmony between clothing and coiffure elevates the storytelling to new heights.

➢ **Broadway Hair as an Art Form**. Broadway hairstylists are not mere technicians; they are artists in their own right. Their work involves a unique blend of creativity and technical expertise, as they sculpt hair into masterpieces that breathe life into characters. It's a celebration of the power of hair to transform, captivate, and inspire.

In this district where dreams take center stage, your hairstyle isn't just an accessory; it's a part of the performance. As the curtains rise and the orchestra plays, remember: Broadway isn't just a place; it's a state of mind. Welcome to the world of Broadway glamour, where your tresses take on a leading role in the drama of Manhattan's most glamorous district.

Completed Tasks: Hairstyles and Hairpiece Activities

Inspirational Quote

FROM A SMALL SEED A MIGHTY TRUNK MAY GROW. — Aeschylus

Action Items: Intentions and Thoughts

The Melting Pot of Manhattan

In the heart of Manhattan, the city that never sleeps, a unique phenomenon unfolds daily—the convergence of cultures, traditions, and identities that shape the world. This living mosaic is reflected not only in the diverse faces that grace its streets but also in the intricate, culturally rich tapestry of hairstyles that adorn its residents.

> ➤ **A Diverse Tapestry**. Manhattan is a microcosm of the world, where people from all corners of the globe converge to chase their dreams. The city's rich tapestry of cultures is reflected not only in its diverse population but also in its myriad of hairstyles. From the intricate braids of Harlem to the sleek bobs of Chinatown, Manhattan's streets are a living showcase of global hairstyling traditions. It's a vibrant celebration of diversity, where every block tells a different story through its inhabitants' hair.

> ➤ **Harlem's Legacy**. Harlem, with its historic significance as a hub of African American culture, has long been a source of inspiration for hairstyling trends. The neighborhood's iconic cornrows, afros, and intricate weaves have transcended local boundaries to become global fashion statements. Explore the evolution of Harlem's hairstyles, from the days of the Harlem Renaissance to contemporary expressions of Black pride and identity through hair. It's a journey through history and heritage, where each hairstyle carries the weight of cultural significance.

> ➤ **Chinatown Chic**. In the heart of Manhattan's bustling Chinatown, a different kind of hairstyling magic unfolds. Traditional Chinese hair accessories, intricate updos, and the art of Feng Tou (hair wrapping) are celebrated here. Delve into the world of Chinatown hairstylists who seamlessly blend ancient traditions with modern aesthetics, creating looks that are as much about culture as they are

176

about fashion. It's an exploration of how hair can serve as a bridge between generations and a testament to the enduring influence of heritage.

➤ **Little Italy's Elegance**. The Italian-American community in Little Italy brings its own flair to Manhattan's hairstyling scene. Classic elegance meets modern trends in this neighborhood, where barbershops and salons have become institutions. From perfectly coiffed pompadours to the timeless allure of the Italian blowout, uncover the secrets of Little Italy's hairstyling traditions. It's a journey through the timeless charm of Italian style, where even a simple haircut is a work of art.

➤ **Global Fusion**. Beyond these distinct neighborhoods, Manhattan is a melting pot of hairstyling influences from around the world. From the intricate henna patterns of South Asian henna artists to the avant-garde hair artistry of avant-garde stylists, explore the global fusion of hairstyling trends that coalesce in this vibrant city. It's a celebration of how Manhattan serves as a crossroads for beauty traditions from every corner of the globe, where diversity is not just embraced but celebrated.

➤ **A Living Canvas**. Manhattan's streets are a living canvas where hairstyling is not just about personal grooming but a form of self-expression, cultural celebration, and artistic innovation. It's a testament to the city's enduring allure as a place where dreams are not just pursued but also reflected in every strand of hair. Manhattan's hairstyling scene is vibrant and ever-evolving.

In this melting pot of cultures and styles, we've witnessed the magic of hairstyling as a means of bridging worlds, celebrating heritage, and expressing individuality. Manhattan's hairstyles are a testament to the power of diversity as a source of inspiration, self-discovery, and artistic innovation.

Completed Tasks: Hairstyling Influences Activities

_____

_____

_____

_____

_____

_____

_____

_____

_____

_____

_____

_____

_____

_____

_____

_____

_____

_____

_____

_____

_____

_____

_____

_____

_____

_____

_____

_____

Inspirational Quote

WHAT LIES BEHIND US AND WHAT LIES BEFORE US ARE TINY MATTERS COMPARED TO WHAT LIES WITHIN US. — Ralph Waldo Emerson

Action Items: Intentions and Thoughts

A Metamorphosis of Style

In the heart of Manhattan, the city that never sleeps, a unique phenomenon unfolds daily—the metamorphosis of style. The bustling streets and glittering skyline of this urban jungle bear witness to the ever-evolving fashion landscape, where personal style is a constant work of art, and reinvention is the name of the game.

➤ **The Power of Personal Expression**. In Manhattan, personal style is more than just clothing; it's a form of self-expression. What you wear is a language that communicates your identity, your aspirations, and your journey through life. Manhattanites understand that fashion is a powerful tool for expressing their individuality and uniqueness.

➤ **The Power of Reinvention**. The city's fast-paced and ever-changing environment encourages reinvention. Whether it's a new hairstyle, a wardrobe makeover, or a daring fashion choice, Manhattanites are unafraid to explore and experiment with their style. It's a city where transformation is not only accepted but celebrated, and fashion plays a pivotal role in this-ongoing process of self-discovery and reinvention.

➤ **Being Fashion-Forward is a Way of Life in Manhattan**. It's about embracing the new, pushing boundaries, and setting trends rather than following them. Whether it's experimenting with bold colors, incorporating vintage classics into modern ensembles, or creating entirely new fashion movements, Manhattanites are at the forefront of the fashion world, constantly shaping the industry's direction.

➤ **A Love Affair with Luxury**. Manhattan sets the standard for luxury fashion. Its upscale shopping districts, including Madison Avenue and Fifth Avenue, are home to world-renowned boutiques and flagship stores. Luxury shopping is not just an activity; it's an experience, and Manhattanites indulge in it with enthusiasm.

➢ **A Hub of Street Style Inspiration**. Manhattan's streets serve as a dynamic source of fashion inspiration for the world. Street style photographers flock to neighborhoods like SoHo, Williamsburg, and the Lower East Side to capture the unique fashion statements of locals. These candid snapshots of individual style often become trendsetters and influence fashion choices worldwide.

➢ **The Power of Accessories**. Accessories are a defining element of Manhattan style. From statement jewelry and high-end watches to designer handbags and bespoke shoes, accessories are the finishing touches that elevate an outfit from ordinary to extraordinary. Manhattanites understand that the right accessories can transform a look and make a powerful fashion statement.

➢ **Fashion as Social Currency**. In Manhattan, fashion is not just a personal expression; it's also a form of social currency. Your choice of clothing, designer labels, and style can open doors, establish connections, and signal your belonging to specific social circles. Fashion is woven into the fabric of social interactions, from high-profile events to exclusive parties and gatherings, where attire plays a significant role in making lasting impressions.

In the labyrinthine streets of Manhattan, style is more than just clothing—it's a reflection of identity, a testament to creativity, and a celebration of diversity. The metamorphosis of style in this vibrant city is a never-ending journey, where reinvention is embraced, personal expression is cherished, and fashion is a work of art that continually redefines itself. Welcome to the ever-evolving world of Manhattan style—a love affair with luxury, a canvas for self-expression, and a constant celebration of the extraordinary.

Completed Tasks: Social Currency Activities

Inspirational Quote

LET LIFE HAPPEN TO YOU. BELIEVE ME: LIFE IS IN THE RIGHT, ALWAYS. —
Rainer Maria Rilke

Action Items: Intentions and Thoughts

Action Items: Intentions and Thoughts

Manhattan's Hair Mavens:
Interviews with the City's Top Stylists

Manhattan, a kaleidoscope of inspirations, where every corner buzzes not just with the chatter of passersby but whispers of stylistic secrets that the city holds close to its heart. Amid its grand theaters and quaint cafes, it isn't merely about living the big city life; it's about defining it—with flair, finesse, and of course, fabulous hair.

Picture this: As you gracefully navigate the labyrinth of the Meatpacking District, it's not the swank of your shoes or the gleam of your accessories that makes heads turn. It's the cascade of your hair, styled by the very best the city has to offer. Darling, that is the true Manhattan Walk of Fame, where each tress is a testament to the city's unending passion for perfection.

In this riveting chapter of The Manhattan Diaries, we peel back the velvet curtain to reveal the magicians behind the most iconic hairstyles of our age. From the understated elegance of the Upper East Side bob to the vibrant hues representing the eclectic East Village, you'll meet the maestros who make magic with their shears and brushes.

However, this story isn't simply about hair—it's about the heartbeat of Manhattan, its spirit. It's about capturing the essence of each neighborhood, each mood, each moment, in a style that's uniquely you. It's a dance between the classic and the contemporary, a romance between the hair and the city it graces.

Journey with me, as we sit in the hallowed chairs of Manhattan's elite salons, listening to tales spun from the very fingers that have shaped the city's style. Because in Manhattan, every hair flip, every curl, every strand is a story waiting to be told. Welcome to The Manhattan Diaries—where your crowning glory can shine as brilliantly as the city's most luminous lights.

The Artistry of Manhattan's Hair Stylists

In the heart of Manhattan, a select group of hairstyling artisans shape the world of fashion and beauty. We delve into The Manhattan Diaries to explore their captivating realm. Each salon offers a unique experience, reflecting the city's ever-evolving realm. Each salon offers a unique experience, reflecting the city's ever-evolving spirit. Join me on this journey into the world of Manhattan's top hairstylists, where every strand tells a diverse story as vibrant as the city itself.

➢ **Iconic Salons of Manhattan**. Manhattan is a city that boasts an impressive lineage of iconic salons, each with its own storied history and unique charm. From the timeless elegance of the Warren-Tricomi Salon in the Plaza Hotel to the avant-garde allure of Sally Hershberger's downtown atelier, these establishments have become landmarks in their own right. Step inside these hallowed halls, where innovation dances with tradition, and where the latest trends are born, and discover the secrets to Manhattan's enduring beauty.

➢ **Styling the Stars**. In a city that never sleeps, stars always need to look their best, and the master stylists of Manhattan have risen to the occasion time and gain. Meet the visionaries behind the scenes who have worked their magic on the tresses of A-list celebrities, transforming them into icons of beauty and glamour. From the sleek bobs that graced the red carpet to the voluminous waves that have cascaded down countless stages, these stylists are the unsung heroes of the city's glittering nightlife.

➢ **Neighborhood Flair**. Manhattan's neighborhoods are as diverse as the people who inhabit them, and its salons are no different. Explore how each salon captures the unique essence of its neighborhood, reflecting the character and spirit of the community it calls home. Whether it's the sleek sophistication of Midtown's high-rises or the artistic eccentricity of the Lower East Side, these salons are more than just places of beauty—they are extensions of the vibrant neighborhoods they serve.

➢ **The Craftsmanship**. Behind every stunning hairstyle is an intricate tapestry of craftsmanship and creativity. Learn about the painstaking techniques and creative processes that go into crafting the perfect coiffure, turning heads on the bustling streets of Manhattan. From precision cutting to expert color blending, these stylists are true artists, sculpting hair into works of art that seamlessly blend form and function.

➢ **Secrets of the Trade**. What sets these master stylists apart? Dive deep into the world of Manhattan's hair elite and uncover the closely guarded secrets of the trade. From the latest trends in haircare to the must-have products that every Manhattanite swears by, these experts share their insights and tips, offering a glimpse into their world of beauty and sophistication. Whether you're a seasoned trendsetter or just looking to elevate your personal style, these insider secrets will inspire and empower you to embrace the Manhattan look with confidence.

➢ **SoHo Sophistication**. SoHo's salons offer a fusion of bohemian charm and urban sophistication. Explore the world of effortlessly chic styles that seamlessly transition from daytime to nighttime.

In the hands of these talented hairstylists, Manhattan's residents and visitors alike become living canvases, their hair transformed into works of art that mirror the city's diverse and dynamic personality. With each flick of a brush and every snip of scissors, these artists create hairstyles that celebrate the essence of Manhattan—an ever-changing, always captivating masterpiece. Welcome to a world where your hair is the canvas, and Manhattan's hairstylists are the artists who paint its story.

Completed Tasks: Secrets of the Trade Activities

_____
_____
_____
_____
_____
_____
_____
_____
_____
_____
_____
_____
_____
_____
_____
_____
_____
_____
_____
_____
_____
_____
_____
_____
_____
_____
_____
_____

Inspirational Quote

THE ONLY WAY TO DISCOVER THE LIMITS OF THE POSSIBLE IS TO GO BEYOND THEM INTO THE IMPOSSIBLE. — Arthur C. Clarke

Action Items: Intentions and Thoughts

Neighborhood-Inspired Styles

In the heart of Manhattan, where the city's eclectic neighborhoods converge, a tapestry of styles unfolds. Each neighborhood boasts its own unique character, its own rhythm, and its own sense of fashion. As the city's fashionistas navigate the bustling streets, they draw inspiration from the vibrant neighborhoods they call home. From the Upper East Side's timeless elegance to the East Village's bohemian chic, Manhattan's neighborhoods are the ultimate source of style inspiration. In this chapter, we delve into the enchanting world of neighborhood-inspired styles, where fashion becomes a reflection of the city's diverse and dynamic spirit.

➢ **Uptown Elegance: The Upper East Side's Timeless Glamour**. The Upper East Side, synonymous with sophistication and refinement, inspires a style that exudes timeless elegance. Discover the allure of classic silhouettes, tailored ensembles, and polished accessories that define the uptown look. Explore how the neighborhood's historic architecture and cultural institutions influence fashion choices, from the Met Gala to high-society soirees.

➢ **Downtown Bohemia: Embracing the East Village Vibe**. The East Village is a haven for the avant-garde, where creativity knows no bounds. Explore the eclectic and unconventional style that defines this neighborhood. Dive into the world of artistic expression, where vintage finds, edgy streetwear, and bold accessories come together to create a unique downtown look. Uncover the influence of local artists, musicians, and the thriving underground scene on fashion trends that challenge the status quo.

➢ **Chelsea Chic: Where Art Meets Fashion**. Chelsea, a neighborhood known for its art galleries and cultural diversity, inspires a style that seamlessly blends artistry and fashion. Explore how the neighborhood's vibrant art scene influences clothing choices, with bold prints, statement pieces, and a touch of bohemian flair. Learn about the fusion of high fashion and street art, where fashionistas draw inspiration from the neighborhood's murals and creative energy.

➢ **Midtown Modernity: The Pulse of Corporate Couture**. Midtown Manhattan is the bustling epicenter of business and commerce, shaping a style that is sleek, professional, and effortlessly chic. Delve into the world of power dressing, where tailored suits, structured silhouettes, and sophisticated accessories reign supreme. Discover how Midtown's towering skyscrapers and corporate culture set the tone for a fashion-forward yet polished look that means business.

➢ **Harlem Renaissance: Celebrating Culture and Heritage**. Harlem's rich cultural heritage and vibrant music scene inspire a style that celebrates diversity, creativity, and self-expression. Explore the influence of African and African-American culture on fashion choices, from colorful prints to bold accessories. Learn about the significance of Harlem's historic landmarks and cultural events in shaping a style that pays homage to its storied past.

In a city that thrives on diversity, each neighborhood tells its own fashion story, inviting residents and visitors alike to embrace a style that resonates with the spirit of the streets they walk. From uptown elegance to downtown bohemia, from Midtown modernity to the cultural celebration of Harlem, Manhattan's neighborhoods are a wellspring of inspiration for the city's fashion-forward denizens. So, whether you're strolling through Central Park or exploring the vibrant streets of the Lower East Side, remember that in Manhattan, style is not just what you wear—it's a reflection of the neighborhood you call home. Welcome to the world of neighborhood-inspired styles in the city that never sleeps.

Completed Tasks: Style Inspiration Activities

Inspirational Quote

LIFE IS NEVER FAIR, AND PERHAPS IT IS A GOOD THING FOR MOST OF US THAT IT IS NOT. — Oscar Wilde

Action Items: Intentions and Thoughts

The Role of Hairstyling in Manhattan's Lifestyle

Manhattan, a city of undeniable charisma, thrives on the dynamism of its residents, and this vibrant energy finds its expression not just in the city's towering skyscrapers but in the art of hairstyling. Each coiffed mane that graces the bustling streets is a statement—a testament to the city's fast-paced lifestyle, ambition, and unyielding pursuit of perfection. In this chapter, we delve into the role of hairstyling in Manhattan's lifestyle, where hair isn't just an accessory; it's an art form, a reflection of the city's spirit.

➤ **Elevating Elegance: The Power of a Well-Groomed Mane**. In Manhattan, appearance matters, and a well-groomed mane is a vital element of one's overall presentation. Whether you're navigating the corporate boardrooms of Wall Street or enjoying a leisurely brunch in the West Village, impeccable hairstyling is non-negotiable. Sleek updos, precision haircuts, and perfectly coiled curls exude a sense of confidence and sophistication. The city's professionals understand that a polished appearance can be a catalyst for success, making hairstyling an essential part of their daily routine.

➤ **Creativity and Self-Expression: Manhattan's Hairstyling Canvas**. Manhattan's diverse and creative population extends its flair to hairstyling. Residents of the city embrace hairstyling as a form of self-expression. From vibrant hair colors that mirror the city's vibrant arts scene to intricate braids that tell stories of cultural diversity, Manhattan's residents aren't afraid to push boundaries. Whether you're in Harlem or the Lower East Side, you'll witness a kaleidoscope of hairstyles that reflect individuality, creativity, and the unapologetic pursuit of uniqueness.

➤ **The Salon Experience: A Manhattan Ritual**. Manhattan's salons aren't just places for haircuts and blowouts; they are sanctuaries of pampering and rejuvenation. Visiting a salon is a cherished ritual for

Manhattanites, offering moments of relaxation and self-care amid their hectic schedules. The city's top stylists and colorists are revered for their expertise, making every salon visit an opportunity to be transformed. It's not merely a haircut; it's a rejuvenation of the soul, a chance to recharge in a city that never sleeps.

➢ **Hair as a Statement: The Manhattan Lifestyle Chronicle**. Beyond aesthetics, hairstyling in Manhattan is a storytelling tool. It's a silent statement that narrates one's journey, ambitions, and aspirations. The choice of hairstyle can reveal a lot about a person's lifestyle and values. In this city, where every step is a part of a larger narrative, every strand of hair is a page in the chronicle of the Manhattan lifestyle. It's about making an impression, leaving a mark, and ensuring that your presence is felt in a city where millions strive to stand out.

➢ **The Signature Mane: A Reflection of Manhattan's Dynamism**. Manhattan, a city of undeniable charisma, thrives on the dynamism of its residents, and this vibrant energy finds its expression not just in the city's towering skyscrapers but in the art of hairstyling. Each coiffed mane that graces the bustling streets is a statement—a testament to the city's fast-paced lifestyle, ambition, and unyielding pursuit of perfection. In this chapter, we delve into the role of hairstyling in Manhattan's lifestyle, where hair isn't just an accessory; it's an art form, a reflection of the city's spirit.

In Manhattan, hair isn't just hair—it's a canvas for self-expression, a reflection of ambition, and a symbol of the city's unstoppable spirit. Whether you're sipping cocktails at a rooftop bar or closing deals in a Midtown office, your hairstyle is your signature, your statement, and your connection to the vibrant lifestyle that defines this remarkable city. Welcome to The Manhattan Diaries, where every strand of hair tells a story as captivating as the city itself.

Completed Tasks: Impeccable Hairstyling Activities

_____
_____
_____
_____
_____
_____
_____
_____
_____
_____
_____
_____
_____
_____
_____
_____
_____
_____
_____
_____
_____
_____
_____
_____
_____

Inspirational Quote

YOU CAN PREACH A BETTER SERMON WITH YOUR LIFE THAN WITH YOUR
LIPS. — Oliver Goldsmith

Action Items: Intentions and Thoughts

Behind the Scenes with Hair Magicians

Manhattan, the epicenter of dreams, ambition, and relentless pursuit of success, is a city that thrives on its unique blend of cultures, personalities, and styles. In the heart of this bustling metropolis, hairstyling is not merely a beauty routine but a vibrant expression of individuality and lifestyle. Every street corner, each upscale salon, and every chic boutique exudes an air of sartorial sophistication that Manhattanites carry with panache. This chapter delves into the intricate role of hairstyling in the tapestry of Manhattan's lifestyle, where hair becomes an emblem of self-expression, a signature accessory, and a reflection of the city's multifaceted charm.

➤ **The Artisans of Avenues**. In the bustling avenues of Manhattan, hairstylists are revered not just as professionals but as true artists. Their salons, scattered across the city from uptown to downtown, function as studios where creativity meets elegance. These hair magicians use their shears and brushes to sculpt looks that are as avant-garde as any piece of art found in nearby galleries, turning each client's hair into a masterpiece reflective of both personal style and the latest trends.

➤ **Cultural Mosaic of Styles**. Manhattan's diversity is its trademark, and this is vividly reflected in its hairstyling. Each neighborhood offers a glimpse into different worlds; from the sleek, straight cuts popular in corporate Midtown, to the bold, expressive styles of Harlem's historic streets. Hairstyling here is not just about beauty but about making a statement of identity, with each style showcasing influences from around the globe.

➤ **Innovation in Technique**. Manhattan's hairstylists are at the forefront of technological innovation and technique in the beauty industry. Utilizing state-of-the-art tools and pioneering new methods, these stylists can offer services ranging from 3D hair printing for precise cuts to personalized hair health diagnostics, ensuring that each client receives not only a stylistic transformation but also a tailored approach to hair care.

➤ **Celebrity Influence**. The impact of celebrity culture on hairstyling trends is pronounced in Manhattan, where the latest celebrity hairstyles are quickly adopted and adapted by local stylists. Whether it's a film premiere or a fashion gala, the hairstyles sported by celebrities often set the benchmark for what's hot, influencing street styles and salon requests across the city.

➤ **Fashion Week Frenzy**. During New York Fashion Week, Manhattan's hairstylists collaborate closely with fashion designers to create influential looks that will set the tone for upcoming seasons. These stylists work under intense pressure and fast-paced environments to deliver innovative and trend-setting styles that complement the high fashion on the runways.

➤ **The Psychological Impact**. A visit to a hairstylist in Manhattan can be transformative, not just physically but emotionally and psychologically. A new hairstyle can significantly boost a person's confidence, enhance their mood, and empower them to present their best self to the world.

In conclusion, hairstyling in Manhattan is more than a beauty ritual; it's a pivotal form of self-expression and cultural identity. The city's skilled stylists not only reflect Manhattan's dynamic fashion landscape but also shape the personal narratives of those who navigate its vibrant streets. Each visit to a Manhattan salon is a transformative experience, reaffirming an individual's connection to the energetic pulse of this iconic city. Thus, in Manhattan, hairstyling is not just about appearance—it's an integral part of the city's life and style.

Completed Tasks: Hair Innovation Activities

Inspirational Quote

IT TAKES HALF YOUR LIFE BEFORE YOU DISCOVER LIFE IS A DO-IT-YOURSELF PROJECT. — Napoleon Hill

MANHATTAN'S HAIR MAVENS

Action Items: Intentions and Thoughts

Action Items: Intentions and Thoughts

City Roundup:
Unraveling the Tresses of Manhattan's Tapestry

In the glittering realm of Manhattan, where city lights paint the sky in a mesmerizing dance, we've embarked on a journey of self-discovery through the art of hairstyling. "Skyline Secrets: How Manhattan's Elite Tame Their Tresses" has been our guide, and together we've uncovered the intricacies of Manhattan's elite and their intimate relationship with their hair. From the Upper East Side elegance to the bohemian spirit of SoHo, from uptown brunches to midnight soirees, we've witnessed how hairstyles not only frame faces but also tell stories, whisper secrets, and unravel inner selves.

In our quest to understand tresses of Manhattan's tapestry, we've learned that hair is more than just a statement; it's an extension of one's identity. Each chapter revealed the intricate tapestry of Manhattan's diverse neighborhoods and their unique influences on style. We've met the magicians behind the scenes, the stylists who sculpt dreams with their shears and brushes, and we've marveled at their artistry.

As we conclude our journey with "City Roundup: Unraveling the Tresses of Manhattan's Tapestry," we realize that the true magic of Manhattan lies not just in its towering skyscrapers or bustling streets, but in the stories woven into every strand of hair, in the conversations sparked by a well-coiffed mane, and in the endless possibilities of self-expression.

May you take the lessons learned from these pages and apply them to your own journey of self-discovery, whether you're strolling down Fifth Avenue or sipping cocktails in a hidden speakeasy. Tresses of Manhattan's tapestry are a mirror reflecting the beauty, diversity, and resilience that reside within each of us. So, let your hair be your guide, your canvas, and your storyteller as you navigate the intricate, enigmatic, and endlessly fascinating world of Manhattan.

1. High-Rise Hairdos: Secrets from Penthouse Salons

In "High-Rise Hairdos: Secrets from Penthouse Salons," we ascend to Manhattan's most illustrious penthouse salons to discover the secrets behind the city's most iconic hairstyles. This chapter of The Manhattan Diaries delves into how the city's elite stylists craft hairdos that are not just styles, but symbols of ambition and identity, inspired by the architectural wonders of Manhattan itself. From the breezy waves of a Central Park stroll to the sleek precision of an uptown bun, each hairstyle is a testament to the city's spirit— a personal blueprint of dreams reaching skyward. Here, every strand tells a story, and every style reflects Manhattan's relentless pursuit of perfection.

2. Fifth Avenue Follies: The Truth About those Lustrous Locks

In "Fifth Avenue Follies: The Truth About those Lustrous Locks," we dive into the exclusive world of Manhattan's elite haircare rituals. This chapter of The Manhattan Diaries reveals the secrets behind the glamorous hairstyles seen on Fifth Avenue, from emergency late-night trims to luxurious conditioning treatments infused with champagne. We explore how these sophisticated styles reflect the city's blend of elegance and ambition, making every hair flip a statement of personal and urban narratives. Join us for an intimate look at the high-life hairstyling that makes Manhattan's lustrous locks a symbol of its vibrant spirit.

3. Cocktail Coiffures: Hairstyles to Sip Martinis In

In "Cocktail Coiffures: Hairstyles to Sip Martinis In," this chapter of The Manhattan Diaries explores the glamorous world of cocktail-hour hairstyles in Manhattan. It highlights styles like the elegant chignon and lively bob, perfect for the city's social scene. Here, hairstyles aren't just about beauty; they're a declaration of presence, embodying Manhattan's dynamic spirit at every upscale bar and street corner. Join us as we uncover how each meticulously crafted hairdo becomes a personal anthem, making every cocktail hour a showcase of style and ambition.

4. The Park Avenue Ponytail: A Twist on the Classic Updo

In "The Park Avenue Ponytail: A Twist on the Classic Updo," this chapter of The Manhattan Diaries delves into the iconic Park Avenue Ponytail, a symbol of Manhattan's elegant yet modern spirit. We explore how this sophisticated hairstyle reflects the city's ambitious ethos and social scene, from its elegantly teased crown to its detailed, ribbon-wrapped ends. This updo is more than just a style—it's a statement, narrating tales of Manhattan's grandeur and the dreams that unfold across its skyline. The Park Avenue Ponytail not only captivates but also embodies the city's narrative, making every wearer a part of Manhattan's storied tapestry.

5. Brunching and Braiding: Uptown Styles for Lazy Sundays

In "Brunching and Braiding: Uptown Styles for Lazy Sundays," from The Manhattan Diaries, we explore how Manhattan's leisurely brunches become showcases for intricate braiding styles. This chapter reveals how hairstyles like elegant waterfall braids and intricate crown plaits are not just fashion statements but narrate the city's vibrant lifestyle. As we journey through Manhattan's salons and brunch spots, each braid emerges as a symbol of personal style and the city's rhythm, proving that even on a lazy Sunday, every twist and turn of your hair tells a compelling story.

6. Met Gala Mystique: The Art of Red Carpet-Ready Tresses

In "Met Gala Mystique: The Art of Red Carpet-Ready Tresses," from The Manhattan Diaries, we delve into the sophisticated hairstyles that illuminate the Met Gala, Manhattan's premier fashion event. This chapter reveals how each carefully crafted hairstyle—be it voluminous waves or avant-garde updos—is a statement of style, synced with the city's pulsating energy. We explore New York's elite salons, uncovering the secrets behind the dazzling hairdos that not only complement the evening's gowns but also make a grand statement on the Met's iconic staircase, showcasing individuality and Manhattan's dramatic flair.

7. SoHo Sleek: Where Bohemian Meets Luxe

In "SoHo Sleek: Where Bohemian Meets Luxe," from The Manhattan Diaries, we explore the distinctive blend of bohemian charm and upscale sophistication that characterizes SoHo. This chapter takes you through its cobbled streets, where fashion ranges from vintage chic to modern luxury, mirroring the neighborhood's artistic roots and affluent presence. We delve into how SoHo's style is not just worn but lived, with each fashion choice echoing the area's vibrant history and urban allure. This journey through SoHo reveals how style and city life intertwine, making every outfit a narrative of Manhattan's evolving cultural tapestry.

8. Midnight Manes: Taming Your Hair for After-Hour Soirees

In "Midnight Manes: Taming Your Hair for After-Hour Soirees," from The Manhattan Diaries, we dive into the art of perfecting hairstyles for Manhattan's electrifying nightlife. This chapter showcases how to style your hair—from sultry curls to sleek buns—that dazzles under the city lights, ensuring each mane makes a bold statement at any late-night event. As you navigate Manhattan's glamorous nocturnal scene, your hair becomes more than just a part of your outfit; it embodies the mystery and allure of the city after dark, making every appearance unforgettable.

9. Brooklyn to Broadway: A Journey of Diverse Hair Inspirations

In "Brooklyn to Broadway: A Journey of Diverse Hair Inspirations," from The Manhattan Diaries, we explore the transformation of hairstyles from

Brooklyn's gritty charm to Broadway's glamorous spotlight. This chapter reveals how diverse styles, from Bed-Stuy braids to dramatic updos, capture the essence of New York's cultural mosaic. Through this journey, hairstyles not only reflect individuality but also the dynamic blend of the city's street art and theatrical flair, showcasing personal transformations that echo the vibrancy of Manhattan and beyond.

10. Manhattan's Hair Mavens: Interviews with the City's Top Stylists

In "Manhattan's Hair Mavens: Interviews with the City's Top Stylists" from The Manhattan Diaries, we meet the master stylists behind Manhattan's iconic hairstyles. This chapter explores how these artisans use their shears and brushes to reflect the city's spirit through diverse hairstyles, from the elegant to the eclectic. As we journey through Manhattan's premier salons, we uncover the passion and artistry that define the city's style scene, showing how each crafted hairstyle is not just a personal statement but a part of Manhattan's vibrant narrative.

Where Do We Go From Here?

As we sweep through the pages of "Skyline Secrets: How Manhattan's Elite Tame Their Tresses," it's impossible not to be dazzled by the sheer spectacle of it all—the intricate dances of hairstylists twirling their magic into every lock, and the elite of Manhattan revealing themselves not just through their achievements but through the very waves and curls that frame their faces. This city, my darling readers, teaches us that our hair, much like our lives, is a canvas ripe for reinvention and expression.

So, where do we go from here, after unraveling the opulent secrets of Manhattan's most privileged? We take our freshly gleaned insights and march forth, coiffed heads held high, into the glaring lights of this city that both judges and embraces with equal fervor.

Next, in our journey is "City-Slick Glamour: Manhattan's Makeup Guide to Mesmerize." If our tresses tell the story of who we are, then our makeup is surely the bold declaration of who we dare to be. Imagine strutting through the pulsing heart of Times Square, your face a masterpiece of confidence, each brushstroke a defiance of the ordinary, a challenge to the mundane.

But before we delve into the vibrant palettes that will adorn our visages, let's pause and reflect on the essence of our metropolitan beautification. Each chapter of this enchanting series is a step, a movement in a grand ballet set against the backdrop of skyscrapers and starlit soirees. We've danced through the salons of the Upper East Side and traced the cobblestones of SoHo with our stylized manes, and now, we're about to face the mirrors of Manhattan's poshest powder rooms.

In Manhattan, beauty isn't just skin deep—it's woven into the very fabric of the city's spirit. As you embark on this next chapter, consider not just the colors you'll choose to adorn your skin, but the parts of yourself you'll daringly reveal to the world. With every swipe of lipstick, every dusting of shadow, you're not merely applying makeup; you're crafting your persona, layer by layer, in the grand theater of urban life.

So, my fabulous voyagers, as we transition from the tresses to the textures of our next grand adventure, remember: Manhattan doesn't just set trends. It sets the stage for transformations. Where we go from here is not just any journey—it's an odyssey of style, a declaration of our inner selves, expressed on the most vibrant canvas of all, our own faces. Welcome to the ongoing saga of The Manhattan Diaries—where you're not just living the story, you're leading it.

Completed Tasks: Recap Activities

Inspirational Quote

WHEN DEEDS SPEAK, WORDS ARE NOTHING. — Pierre-Joseph Proudhon

Action Items: Intentions and Thoughts

Journal Pages: Pen Your Tales

Journal Pages: Pen Your Tales

Journal Pages: Pen Your Tales

Journal Pages: Pen Your Tales

Journal Pages: Pen Your Tales

Journal Pages: Pen Your Tales

Journal Pages: Pen Your Tales

Journal Pages: Pen Your Tales

Journal Pages: Pen Your Tales

Journal Pages: Pen Your Tales